Why She Won't™

Sleep With You Anymore*
*and how you can change that—fast!

The tell-all guide to
getting your woman back in bed
(For men who can't wait one more minute!)

Stephany Ekman

Copyright © 2012 Stephany Ekman Productions
All rights reserved.

No part of this book may be reproduced or transmitted in any form by any means: graphic, electronic or mechanical including photocopying, recording, taping, or by any information storage or retrieval system, without permission in writing from the publisher at info@annandalepress.com.

Cover Illustration: © Michael Crawford/ The New Yorker Collection / www.cartoonbank.com

Cover Design: Scott Rovin

Interior Design: Katherine Grayson

Why She Won't™ is a trademark of Stephany Ekman Productions

ANNANDALE PRESS

Printed in the United States
First Printing

*For all the men who are confounded by their women,
and all the women who have been waiting
for their men to figure them out.*

CONTENTS

Introduction - I'm Here, You're Here	1
Part I — Precisely Why She Won't	6
1 - What If She Doesn't Like Sex?	7
2 - Help! It's a Sexual Stalemate	10
3 - The Way We Were	15
4 - A Conversation Over Coffee	23
5 - The Truth About Men	29
6 - The Truth About Women	35
Part II — Change That, Fast	51
7 - Fanning Her Flames of Sexual Response	52
8 - Magical Thinking vs. Active Loving	55
9 - How to Actively Love and Value	66
10 - Beauty and Desirability = Sex	78
11 - Love and Sex, Strength and Power	83
12 - The Nearness (The Maleness!) of You	89
13 - The Happiness of Pursuit	96
14 - The Importance of Seducing Your Woman, and How to Do It Right	101
15 - What's Her Fantasy? (And Why You Should Care—a LOT)	116
16 - Your Tick List: The 15 Fundamentals	142
Appendix - Not Tonight; Headache	145
Notes	153

Introduction
I'm Here, You're Here

You are not alone.

> An astounding 88 percent of marriages (read: long-term relationships) describe themselves as 'low-sex' partnerships where once-frequent sex occurs rarely or never.

Numerous studies conducted over the past decade have ranked the prevalence of no- or low-sex marriage at around 15 to 20 percent of all marriages, which would indeed make you feel as though you're in a sad minority. But OMG: a recent (2011-2012) online poll of over 18,000 participants[1] revealed that an astounding 88 percent of surveyed marriage partners (and I would argue this applies to long-term relationship partners, as well) describe themselves as in "low-sex" partnerships: relationships where sex that was once a substantial component of the bond, now occurs infrequently or not all. The poll is ongoing. So it appears, my friend, as though you are not so alone in your misery.

Though relationships where the female partner is the one shut out are on the rise, the numbers continue to point to the male as the partner more often "going without." Either way, in low-sex relationships, one partner is identified as the non-participant, while the other partner is identified as (how shall I put this?) still praying for participation. That would be you.

If you are reading this book, you are most probably the male of our species (given the title of this guide). But you may instead be the non-participating female, presented with this information by your mate, in order to re-cement an eroding physical and romantic relationship. (Sort of a "Is this how you feel?" entreaty from your man, which should indicate to you that he will now do just about anything to get you back in bed—including read a self-help book cover-to-cover, and then beg you to read it, too.) You may even be a female who purchased this book for your mate, in a last-gasp attempt to help him to understand just what's preventing you from jumping into the sack more often, or at all.

Whether you are male or female, this may be your first foray into the self-help section of your local conventional or favorite online bookstore, or you may have read just about every advice blog you can get your hands on, in order to re-take that steel fortress once known as the other side of the bed. But the fact of the matter is, it doesn't matter how you got here or who paid for the advice. This is help you haven't seen before.

> **When it comes to long-term relationships, it seems as though each gender has been put together in a manner specifically designed to frustrate the other.**

Why Did I Write This Book?

I wrote *Why She Won't Sleep with You Anymore* because I've always been fascinated by the low- or no-sex predicament many men and women find themselves in when they are in relationships for any length of time. For decades, I've wanted to unravel these mysteries, for sometimes it seems as though—when it comes to long-term relationships—each gender has been put together in a manner specifically designed to frustrate the other! Our instincts and libidos seem well-designed for *initial* courtship, mating and procreating, but enduring physical relationships are more of a challenge to so many.

I wrote this book because I discovered that although there are plenty of advice and psychology books about sex, performing sex, improving sex, increasing sex—and just plain sex, sex, sex, there was virtually nothing out there that spoke to the particular root issues I tackle here. I wrote *Why She Won't* because most advice books about no- or low-sex issues are either written *for* men *by* men attempting to decode the female psyche, or else they are penned by clinicians: psychiatrists, psychologists, family or sex therapists and the like.

> **Lucky you: I am a woman willing to reveal what is *really* going on with females—as unpopular, un-feminist, and embarrassing as these revelations may be to us.**

I take another approach entirely. I am a writer—by trade a decoder of human behavior and a contemplator of love, romance, sexuality and conflict. I am also a twice-married female who, over her lifetime, has had no end of married, divorced, and married-again friends, both female *and* male, most of whom, at one time or another, have wondered aloud about why their once flourishing sex lives were suffering from low-sex-itis.

I'll admit it: I am endlessly intrigued by the dance of the sexes. Why do some relationships work while others flounder? Why do some people sabotage their own happiness while others unwittingly stumble on their joy?

Why She Won't Sleep with You Anymore is the result of many years of candid and confidential conversations with everyday ordinary people just like you, plus queries to countless others and endless online research and blog/chat room monitoring (and you know how addictive that can be!). It is the result of many years of anecdotally (unscientifically) evaluating the patterns that keep emerging from everyday relationship conflicts, and many years of watching what happens when those patterns are purposely and *purposefully* altered.

I believe that men, in particular, do not need yet another male theorizing about the inner workings of the female psyche. In fact, each time I pick up a male-authored advice column or scan a male-penned blog about how to live with and love the opposite sex, I can't help but feel that the (no doubt well-intentioned) advice makes matters worse—it's almost like a Frenchman traveling to China to teach Chinese!

> **Many women are deeply miserable with the 'other' side of the low-sex predicament: They're in a box—and they hammered in a good number of the nails themselves.**

I say: It's lucky for you, the male readers of this book, that I am a woman! More to the point, I am a woman willing to explore what is really going on with the female of our species—as unpopular, un-feminist, and even embarrassing as some of these revelations may be to those of my gender. I'm willing to help men step inside the deepest reaches of the feminine mystique because as frustrated as a man may be by his lack of physical connectedness to his mate, that's how deeply miserable his lady may be with the flip side of their low-sex predicament: She's in a box she doesn't know how to get out of, and she hammered in a good number of the nails herself.

What's Different About *Why She Won't*?
Why She Won't is not another sexual technique book. It is not about what's going right or wrong once you're in the sack together. It's all about what's going wrong *before* you end up (or rather, *don't* end up) in bed. In Part I you'll discover many probable reasons for your current sexual standoff with your lady, and in Part II you'll get easy-to-use solutions to end that stalemate quickly.

In addition, make sure that you carefully review "Not Tonight; Headache," the special Appendix in the back of this book, that details numerous other common causes of diminished sexual interest for women. Even if everything you read in Parts I and II rings true for you, "Not Tonight; Headache" is vital information you absolutely should not miss.

This is a little book, purposely designed to get you to your solutions quickly. But please do take the time to read both Parts I and II, for without the essential discussions in Part I, Part II's action plan could leave you "going through the motions" without any real understanding of where you've gone wrong previously, and where you'll doubtless encounter a roadblock again.

And the truth of the matter is, when it comes to sex, you've had enough of "going through the motions," haven't you? I say it's time for real knock-your-socks-off love and sex again.

Part I – Precisely Why She Won't

Chapter 1
What If She Doesn't Like Sex?

There's an old (not-so-funny) joke I once heard about a boy who kept bringing home terrible grades on his homework, tests and report cards. His family agonized over the possible causes of the dismal marks.

"Maybe he's got that—whatdya call it—dyslexia thing, and so he can't read properly," the boy's father suggested at a family pow-wow about the problem.

"No," sighed the mother. "Little Johnny's been tested, and he's fine. But maybe he's depressed about something," she wondered aloud.

"Depressed?" scoffed his aunt, "Why, the boy whistles all day, happily climbs trees and plays sports with his friends! That boy's not depressed!"

"Then he's not eating enough good, fresh food," decided the child's grandmother. "Or maybe he doesn't sleep well."

"No, no, no—he eats like a horse and sleeps like a lamb," the mother insisted. "I just can't *imagine* why little Johnny isn't doing well in school!" she cried out in frustration.

The grandfather, who had been quietly following the discussion, finally put down his pipe and said, "Did it ever occur to any of you that little Johnny is stupid?"

Genuine Disinterest in Sex

Any time I've had a discussion with a male friend about the underlying causes of a barren sex life, the obvious question always cropped up, sooner or later: *Do many women simply not like sex?* But here, in this book where we're being utterly frank, I will go even further and ask the second and third questions: *And do women instinctively know how to hide that unsavory reality before men commit to them? Do they reveal the truth bit by bit, only after they have a man hooked?*

> **Do many women simply not like sex? And worse, do they instinctively know how to hide that unsavory reality until they have a man hooked?**

My own honest response to both questions is this: There may be some women who, for whatever reason—painful health issues, childhood issues, sexual traumas, gender confusion, religious upbringing—simply do not like sex or want to partake of it. (There are men who feel this way too, by the way.) And there certainly are women who marry men knowing or suspecting that they will not be able to share a normal sex life with their mates. (Men also have been guilty of such deceptions.) So, you have the right to ask a woman the first question, but you'll never get an honest answer to the second and third.

Still, I would be careful about asking your woman if she does not particularly like sex, for she may not like it *now*, as things stand with you both. Furthermore, depending upon how long it's been since the two of you connected carnally, she may not have a clear memory of how much she may once have enjoyed it. (Divorce-hearing dockets are crammed with cases of "disinterested" wives involved in raging affairs after near lifetimes of sexually empty marriages—and the same holds true for "detached" men.)

Resolving that a wife or girlfriend who doesn't sleep with you *must* be frigid can only result in the waste of a warm body and a lifetime of love. For if your mate clearly enjoyed sex with you once upon a time (and you have checked out all the obvious health-related, weight-gain, exhaustion and dysfunctional relationship causes you should absolutely review in the special Appendix, "Not Tonight; Headache"), then you can safely assume that, somewhere inside, your lady does want to enjoy a fulfilling physical life with you again, even if right now she fears that ship has sailed.

> **If your mate clearly enjoyed sex with you once upon a time, then you can safely assume that, somewhere inside, she wants that life with you again.**

What's more, if you are reading this book, something inside of you is convinced that the woman you once so happily bedded (and who so enthusiastically made love to you right back) is still in there somewhere, and you just haven't solved the mystery of what changed and why.

Let's solve that mystery now.

Chapter 2
Help! It's a Sexual Stalemate

Okay: It's nice to know that you are not alone; that countless long-term, committed relationships between men and women have recently been revealed to be low sex partnerships: In other words, that many, many guys just like you are not getting any lately, either. Still, these things don't just happen overnight. Or do they?

Things Just Seemed to Change...
How did this state of affairs creep into *your* long-term relationship? Was there a perceptible change? Did a particular event precede the change in your sexual relationship? Overnight changes are not only more dramatic, they're easier to trace and easier to work on, for both partners can point to a cause and try to work through it.

> Ah, the old stall-until-he-falls-asleep ploy: She's just washing up before bed, but darn if that ritual doesn't take longer every night...

Most often, though, men and women alike say their sexual situation changed gradually, often imperceptibly. Is that the case with you and your mate? Briefly (and feel free to substitute your own scenarios for any of the ones I suggest here), somewhere along the way, the spontaneous sex disappeared and sex became more routine. Before you knew it, sex occurred in bed only; in bed on Saturday nights; in bed on one Sunday morning a month; in bed on birthdays and holidays only; in bed on Armistice Day (do we still celebrate Armistice Day?). Well, you get the picture. Then:

- **Getting her to bed got more and more complicated.** There were just so many things getting in the way! She had a sudden headache; her period; a stomachache; a bad day. She was dealing with the kids, job, dogs, relatives and the state of world affairs. She wasn't in the *mood*. She had to do the laundry, take a bath, clean the kitchen, call a friend. Good Lord, she just slept with you a month ago!

- **She *said* she was coming to bed, but you fell asleep** before she did (you clod). Ah, the old stall-until-he-falls-asleep ploy. Why does this happen so often? She'll tell you that she was busy in the bathroom with some of the items in the above paragraph (world affairs always held *me* up). Or maybe she was simply going through her pre-bed wash-up routine, but darn if that ritual doesn't take longer every night.

- **She verbally agreed to sex, but an argument ensued.** Hey, you can't expect her to want to sleep with you when you've gotten her all upset (about the kids, house, dogs, TV remote, etc.), can you? She was even undressed and ready to join in, but then you had to go and do something that you *know* is a big turn-off for her. (Breathing, maybe.)

- **She was willing, but it just isn't happening "right"** anymore. It was a Saturday night or that long-awaited Sunday morning (or Armistice Day). The kids were off on sleepovers (or her gym was closed, her hair salon shut down, or her girlfriends were out of town), and you gave her that "It's Sunday morning and you've got no excuses—let's see you wriggle out of *this* one" look, and so she acquiesced.

  Yet, before you knew it, there were problems: The room was too warm or cold; she forgot to thoroughly brush her teeth or take the pill; she needed to let the cat in. No problem: You quickly adjusted the thermostat, brought her a glass of mouthwash and her pill, and in one swift move leapt over the kitchen counter to unlock the back door and let the cat in. All was well again. But then, back in the sack, things started to go south—and not in a good way. Your arm was in the way; you didn't shave again; you stroked her too hard, too gently, not at all. Then you rushed through foreplay; spent too long on foreplay; moved things along too quickly and she wasn't ready yet; or took so long that she was no *longer* ready. And so on and so on. It was clear that circumstances weren't cooperating, or...

- **(Horrors!)** *You* **just don't do it right anymore.** And that seems so strange when, once upon a time, you could do no wrong. Yet you can't help but think that your techniques or your willingness to please haven't changed all that much over the weeks, months or years—have they?

It's Not You, It's Her

At some point or another, especially if your partner is a perfectly decent female human being, she will try to keep from adding insult to injury and explain to you that the fact that the two of you no longer have sex (or much sex, or have lousy sex) has nothing to do with you: It's HER.

> Is it *really* 'Not you, it's her'?
> Or are there graver issues at hand?

She may, in fact, give you a legitimate explanation of what's going on with her, which may include things I refer to in the Appendix discussion: She may indicate that the problem is her health, her weight, fatigue that is not resolving, or a much deeper problem with your relationship that is getting in the way of her feeling genuine love and caring (and thus, an ability to engage in sex).

If even one corner of your gut tells you that there might possibly be a grain of truth in what she says, you should be grateful for her frank admission and your new insight, and express your willingness to focus on those issues immediately. (The Appendix, "Not Tonight; Headache" will help you do just that.)

But sometimes your gut may be sending you nagging little messages that tell you that what you're really getting from her is the classic "It's not you, it's me" line because:

a) **She's *afraid* to tell you** what's really going on in your relationship.

b) **She doesn't *know*** what's really going on in your relationship; she just knows that something is amiss and that sex is the last thing she is in the mood for these days, or—

c) **There are much graver issues at hand** and it's time to head to the marriage counselor or consider time apart.

In my experience, A and B come way before C, so the first or second time you get the "It's not you, it's me" line, the two of you need to have the frankest discussion possible before things go too far off course and move on into the C arena. If that discussion doesn't happen (or even if it does) you still need to read the rest of this book quickly, to stay out of the dreaded C zone!

It's Not Me, It's Us
If your lady is willing to discuss any type of perceived sexual incompatibility with you, be brave! You'd be a fool not to at least urge her to be *gently* candid with you about your lovemaking, and about anything that might be turning her off, driving her away, or needing some improvement.

> Most men swear they'll do or change any sexual technique, if it means that they will have more or better sex with their partner. So why not alter a *non*-sexual technique?

In fact, most men swear that they will do or change *anything* in bed, if it means that they will have more and better sex with their partner. I, for one, believe they are sincere, and most women will believe it too, when it's put just that way.

But if you are changing everything you or she can think of and it only helps temporarily before you are back to Square One again, then I can guarantee you that the cause of her sexual disinterest (or her inability to respond to your efforts) does not lie in what you are doing sexually or the *way* in which you are doing it. If it did, I would have written one of the thousands of books out there about the kinds of activities that happen once couples are *in* bed. Instead, I have written this book, which is all about how to transform your partner into a woman who is more than eager to get *back* into bed with you; to happily join you for whatever ride you take her on and cheerfully (even lustily) take you on some of her own choosing, as well.

> It's not about what's going wrong once you're in bed together. It's about what's going wrong *way before* you get there.

In short: Much of this guide is not about what's going wrong once you are *in* the sack together. It is all about what's going wrong *way before* you end up there—to put it simply, it's all about the underlying reasons for your current sexual stalemate.

Happily, though, your love life with your sweetheart didn't start out as a stalemate, and that's the best news ever, for it means that there exists a very real state of sexual bliss you can return to, if you can figure out how. It's sort of like when your computer files get all corrupted, and you search for the "Restore" program that will get you back to the way things were before that dreaded virus set in. One caveat to the computer restore process however: First, you have to know *what state* you want to return to. In other words: When were things the way they should be? Was it yesterday, or the yesterday before then?

Frankly, it's precisely the same process when you're trying to get back to a state of delight with your lady: A little jog of the memory just may be in order.

Chapter 3
The Way We Were

Once upon a time, a dashing young man (you) came upon a lovely young—or younger than she is now—thing (her) and something inside you began to stir. Perhaps it was the way she smiled at you; maybe it was the sound of her laughter or the sparkle in her eyes when you first spoke to her. Possibly, she feigned disinterest (or actually *was* disinterested, at first) and you took that as a challenge to be met; a mountain to be scaled.

> **Whatever the initial spark, you wanted this alluring damsel, and so you found yourself pursuing her.**

Whatever the initial spark, the fact is that you wanted this alluring damsel, and whether or not you had a chance to examine your motives (probably not), you found yourself pursuing her. Then…

You asked her out. You called her on the phone. You emailed or texted her. You took her to brunch, lunch or dinner; to movies, concerts, or the theater. The two of you went hiking, rollerblading, antiquing. Maybe money was tight and you just hung out together going for walks, watching DVDs (or videos), lying on the sofa talking for hours, making popcorn or warming up pizzas.

Maybe you originally discovered each other in the workplace and so caught fleeting glimpses of each other during the day, then met up for lunch off-site so no one would know you were dating against company rules. Maybe, even, you stole forbidden moments behind copiers, in a supply closet, or in your car when you simply couldn't stand to be apart for a full eight hours.

No matter your story, and whether you knew it or not at the time, the fact of the matter was: You were instinctively "courting" the object of your affection.

> **Whether you knew it or not at the time, you were instinctively 'courting' the object of your affection.**

Biology Came Naturally

Back then, without any training whatsoever, you were performing an eons-old, biologically determined mating dance for your lady love. You were showering her with attention and making her the focus of your every waking moment. (Okay, maybe not *every* waking moment: A guy has to work, go to the gym, hang out with buddies, change his engine oil and do other vital things.)

But I will wager that while you were on that treadmill at the gym or changing your engine oil, you were daydreaming about your girl and maybe even texting or calling her, just to get her response or hear her voice. I'll even bet that while you were hanging out with your friends, you were either discussing your new romance ad nauseam, or else your friends were trying to get information out of you, and you were grinning like a fool. And speaking of fools, I'll also bet that during those early but serious dating days, you did just about anything you could to impress your sweetheart—including spend money you didn't actually have in hand, or act like a buffoon just to make her laugh and see the light in her eyes directed back at *you*.

Fortunately, as the gods would have it, she did think you were funny. And fascinating. And charming. And masterful. And sexy.

And, eventually, she slept with you. Or rather, you enthusiastically slept with each *other*, both reveling in the rapture of those days of mutual discovery. You shared heat and hormones, lust and love. And somewhere along the way, whether you were aware of it or not, you began to build trust between you, cementing the relationship or at least keeping it tacked together as it progressed.

> **Back then, you convinced her she could trust you not just to *say* you loved her, but to *act* in a loving and affectionate manner.**

Love Was an *Action*
By your *actions*—your intense interest in her; your unmistakable pursuit of her; your attention to what she said, did, thought or believed; your obvious need to connect with her, impress her, please her, do for her, *value* her—you eventually convinced her that she could trust you with her heart. That she could trust you not just to *say* that you love her, or profess that you *feel* love for her, but to *act* in a loving, caring and affectionate manner.

So you began to realize that you loved her and, happily, she was loving you right back. There was a lot of talking and discovering, and much deep gazing into each other's eyes. There was touching, hugging, kissing, foreplay, and out-and-out damn good sex going on. And even if it wasn't the best sex of your life (and it may have been; we're just trying to be realistic here), it was good, it was frequent, it was spontaneous, and it felt to you pretty much like what being loved was all about.

> **There was touching, kissing, and damn good sex going on—and it was frequent, spontaneous and felt to you pretty much like what being loved was all about.**

Clearly, this woman cared for you and wanted to be close to you in a way that made you feel wonderful, confident, happy, and desired. She *wanted* to be connected to you on the most intimate level. Intuitively, you began to trust her with your own heart, too.

By her *actions*, she had transmitted to you that she was deeply affected by you.

Then the two of you declared to each other that you were in love. Another step in trust-building: I love you enough to lay myself bare, admit my vulnerability and *tell* you that I love you and that I want us to have some kind of future together.

Along the way, you felt the need to show each other, in any number of ways, that you felt love for one another and wanted to make each other happy. Maybe she cooked for you (labor-of-love action) to see that look of deep satisfaction on your face as you realized that she had spent time and effort to please you. Perhaps you bought her little or even not-so-little gifts (purchasing action), to surprise and delight her.

Possibly, you left little notes for each other (lovey-dovey actions) when you were away, or sent cards to each other (more lovey-dovey actions) for no occasion at all. You may have texted her (messaging action) all during her work day; she may have responded with love notes or emails (more messaging action). You may have fixed her car for her (physical labor action); she may have bought you a cool leather jacket for a special occasion (dress-up-your-man action). You may have taken flowers to her when she wasn't feeling well (sweet and thoughtful action); she may have massaged your back after a long day of lifting and hauling on the job (ah-that-feels-good action).

In between all of this active caring for each other, there was probably a good deal of talking, discussing, sharing, commenting, *noticing* action. You may have picked up on the fact that she got grumpy when she was hungry; she may have noted that you needed decompression time after a particularly tough day. She may have remarked that she loved your saunter and could pick you out in a crowd just by the way you moved; you may have gazed at her one night and told her that she had the most beautiful hair you'd ever seen and that it always smelled like summer, to you. She may have confided that the flash of your smile turned her on; you may have told her that her eyes were a softer brown than any you had ever known.

In those early days, you were letting each other know that you were truly *seeing* each other. More than that, you wanted each other to know that you were appreciating what you saw. You were connecting intimately, familiarly, as thoroughly as you knew how. (Or else you were eagerly learning, on the fly, how to connect in that way.) For some reason, you *needed* to connect that way. You needed to *know* her. You needed to be *known by* her.

And you were truly engaged with each other, wherever you went; seeing a movie and discussing it together; going out with another couple and chatting about their relationship afterward; window shopping while sharing your tastes and dreams.

I'm not surmising that *all* of these actions took place, or even that these *precise* actions occurred. But, hopefully, some of these "love actions"—or actions like them—happened. If they didn't, stop right here, for you may have never made an initial love connection in the first place, and it's going to be mighty hard to reignite a connection you never, for whatever reason, forged.

> **You'll need to change assumptions you've held since she said 'I love you.' Then you can alter your behavior so that, like magic, *she will alter hers.***

Yet, if any part of my little story rings true or sends you back longingly to days gone by, then I promise you, you can find your girl again and quickly rebuild a solid, rewarding, unshakable sex life with her. And you *won't* need to recreate your entire dating past and turn back into a starry-eyed 20-something. (At least, not if you don't want to.)

Change Is In *Your* Hands

To start, however, you *will* need to understand what was actually behind the initial process that brought you together in the first place. Then you will need to change some basic—but definitely erroneous—male assumptions you've carried with you like old shoes ever since she gave you her heart and said, "I love you." You will need to understand what has happened to her (and your own) thought processes and behaviors, ever since.

Then you will need to alter your own behavior accordingly so that, like magic, *she will alter hers.*

You're Not the Same People

The fact of the matter is that the way you both are now is simply not The Way You Were, and that's a truth you will need to accept if you are to reignite the passion between you. In the whirlwind of new love, everything is fresh and exciting and—for lack of a better phrase—both individuals are basically flying by the seats of their pants, on instinct alone.

That, in itself, is enough to keep sexual anticipation pulsating madly as two lovers vibrate as one—wanting the same things, needing the same things, hoping for the same things.

But the truth is, you are not the same happily oblivious couple you once were: You have been two adult people "working" a relationship for some time now—and in the *real* world, it's hard work much of the time!

Importantly, you also are not the same people in the sense that you are not "one and the same"—you are two distinct individuals of opposite sexes with very differing needs. While those differences can certainly get swept away in the initial stages of romance, sometime afterward they reassert themselves and demand to be accorded true respect.

So, although you may have put off the inevitable for months, years or even decades, if you wish to rediscover your physical life together, you *will* need to consider a number of gender-alien concepts that (though they were once instinctual) now feel unfamiliar to you. Ironically, you will also need to technically *re*-learn many of the things that had once come to you so spontaneously, while you were dating your sweetheart.

It may be quite a long time since you've had to examine your own behavior and also attempt to see some things from the inside of your lady's little head (and maybe you've never felt compelled to do either of these things). After all, when you were dating each other and were caught up in the first throes of love, you didn't have to; it seemed as though the two of you wanted all of the same things.

Back then (while you were so immersed in each other and she even seemed to like everything you liked) you may have believed that simply transferring onto your partner the things that made *you* happy, would work equally well for *her*. Maybe you believe that even now? After all, it's such a simple, comfortable approach.

> **You believed that transferring onto your girl the things that made *you* happy, would work equally well for *her*. Wrong!**

The problem is, in the real world of grown-up love and sex, "transference" could be your absolutely worst approach. Once more: Don't take it personally! The fact of the matter is that:

A woman's needs can be entirely different from those of a man, especially when it comes to physical and emotional love.

Again: She is not like YOU. If you can accept this as a truth, it will be your first step toward removing your forehead from that brick wall you've been slamming it against for so many weeks, months, or years.

> Your goal from here on in is to better understand what truly makes a *woman* (not you; not a MAN) happy in a love relationship. Master those skills and the sex roars back.

Your New Objective

To put it simply, your goal from here on in is to better understand what truly makes a *woman* (not *you*; not a *man*) happy in her love relationship. You'll need to learn or relearn those skills, and then get better at "internalizing" them (making them more instinctive) so that your lady will react more positively to you, and romps in bed will return on a regular basis. How frequent, unmentionable and unimaginable those romps become, is all up to *you*.

Chapter 4
A Conversation Over Coffee

"I just don't understand it," my friend's husband admitted to me at a local coffee joint, late one summer night. The couple had been struggling with their relationship and he had asked for another woman's perspective, so (with my friend's blessing) I said I would be happy to meet with him and help if I could.

"I Do Everything She Asks..."
He confided: "She's so picky these days and never seems happy with anything I do." For instance, he explained, she insisted that if he just helped around the house, their "relationship" would be better. (Translation: She might sleep with him again.) "I try to do what she asks me to," he said, "but then something else pops up that's wrong. So I try to fix that, too, but nothing changes; she still seems unhappy about so many little things. She wasn't like this when we started out, but now the things that bother her just don't seem to end."

> When women get demanding, they actually 'grab at straws.' That is, they don't *know* what is making them unhappy. Luckily, you *will* know and will fix things quickly.

"If she's like me," I offered, "when she gets that way she may not even know why she's being so nit-picky. So she keeps reaching for things she thinks might make her happier, but she's grabbing at straws."

"Well, if *she* doesn't know what she wants, how am I supposed to know?" he insisted. Then he asked the Big Question:

"What Does She Actually Want From Me?"

"Look at it this way," I said to him. "If she's complaining that you never clean up after yourself in the kitchen, you might try to clean it better, to make her happy. But do you honestly think a clean kitchen is the thing that will make her want to sleep with you again?" That solution suddenly seemed ridiculous to us both.

> **If you clean the kitchen to make her happy, do you honestly think that's the thing that will make her want to sleep with you again?**

"If it's not the things she *says* she wants, then what *is* it?" He pleaded. "Tell me and I'll do it! I just want things the way they used to be."

I thought for a moment. "Maybe she's just not feeling loved," I wondered out loud.

"What??" he cried. "I tell her I love her all the time, and she *still* avoids sex or else just goes through the motions." It was clear he was frustrated.

"Technically, 'going through the motions' is still sex," I offered.

"I don't want 'technically,'" he protested. "I don't want her to go through the motions. I want her to *want* to make love to me. I want it to be the way it used to be, or even somewhere near it."

I recalled recent "girl talks" with his wife, my friend. Then I said, "I think you and she want the same things. She wants you to be 'with' her, too, and not just going through the motions. She wants you to *want* to be with her. She wants things the way they once were, too, or anywhere close to it. She loves you but she also needs to feel loved in the way that means something to *her*."

"But I DO love her!" he fairly exploded.

> "I don't want her to go through the motions," he said. "I want her to *want* to make love to me. I want things the way they used to be."

"That's an emotion, not an action," I said, getting out of his way as I said it.

"But I *show* her I love her! I do whatever she asks! If she asks me to run errands for her, help her straighten up the house, or buy some new earrings she's wanted, I do it!"

I decided then to take a chance, in order to make a point. "She can do what *you* ask, too," I reminded him: "She can lie down on the bed—"

For a second there, I thought he was going to throw his coffee cup at me. But he just stared at me across the table until finally, his expression softened.

"You're saying we each need the other not just to *feel* love for us, but to *show love in a way that has meaning to the other person.*"

I nodded.

He went on. "You're saying those ways are very different for each of us."

I told him that they were.

"And clean kitchens and new earrings are nice to have, but it's not really what she needs most, when it comes to feeling loved by me. Right?"

"Yes," I said. Then he asked me why his working hard for the things they needed didn't make her feel loved. "Doesn't that show her that I love her?" he wanted to know.

That's when I asked him if *her* hard work at her job made *him* feel loved the way he needed to feel loved. And I asked him if the fact that she cooked dinner for him or did his laundry for him made him feel the way he did when she was in bed with him.

"But doesn't my *physically* wanting her show her how much I love her?" he asked.

At that point, I could only tell him how I myself felt in such circumstances. "Sometimes it does," I said. But I had to break it to him that women are just not as physically 'on' all the time, the way men are. *"Women just aren't men,"* I told him.

"I know, I know," he said.

"No: REALLY," I insisted. "Maybe you're thinking that what works with you *should* work for her, but it simply doesn't." If it did, I told him, women would be glued to porno websites and men would be reading romance novels. *That* got his attention.

> **Maybe you're thinking that what works for *you*, should work for *her*. If that were true, women would be glued to porno sites and men would be reading romance novels.**

We finally got to the heart of the matter when he confessed that he was just plain worried that he didn't know what *would* work for her, or that he didn't know *how* to love her the way she needed to be loved. "It's so much easier for men," he admitted. "All you have to do is be our friend, feed us once in a while, and make love to us like you mean it, as often as possible. Honestly! We'll even be fine when you don't *completely* mean it but you're happy to try. As long as we know you *usually* mean it."

I couldn't help but laugh. "Men are infinitely easier," I granted him. "It's not too hard to mistake what it is you want!"

"It's unfair," he said. "It's so easy for women to know what *we* want, and so hard for us to know what *they* want. Even *they* have trouble understanding it or explaining it!"

I agreed that that was absolutely true. Yet, on the other hand, I explained to him, I had often told my own husband precisely what I needed, and could tell at once that it didn't sound like anything too important to him. At other times, it was clear to me that he thought I was just whining or complaining. "So either our men don't *know* how to respond to us," I put it bluntly, "or else they think we're just being 'silly' or not truly serious."

"Think about it," I asked: "How recently have you heard 'We don't spend time together anymore,' or 'You never say I look pretty'?"

> **You will probably realize that she *did* ask you to give her precisely what she needed— it just didn't sound like anything important to you, so you thought she was not serious.**

There was a pause, and his eyes widened. "*That* was her telling me what she needed in order to feel loved? That sounded like she was telling me I don't do anything right!"

"I know," I sighed. "We women are our own worst enemies. We can't say to you, 'I need my husband to not play golf on Saturday and to spend some time holding hands with me or having lunch with me, or sharing our thoughts like he used to want to do with me.' We can't say to you, 'I want to always feel like your beautiful princess, the way I used to.' It's too embarrassing for us to ask for what you used to give us willingly. So it comes out like some kind of pitiful gripe, and *you* end up feeling like you don't measure up as a husband or boyfriend," I admitted. "And *we* end up alone feeling ugly and undesirable on a Saturday while you play golf or basketball or work on your car.

"Then you come back later on and try to get close to us in the way you know best—physically—and can't understand why we're miserable and resentful. And the following Saturday when you figure you might as well have some fun playing golf again since you're feeling rejected at home, the whole thing starts over again."

He looked stunned. "We simply don't understand what you women need, do we?" he asked.

"Nope," I said. "Not by a long shot."

Chapter 5
The Truth About Men

Before we head into the deepest recesses of the female mind and help you return your mate to a physically loving state, I'd like to take this chapter to lay out some important groundwork. So, don't skip this information about the *male* psyche! You are going to need it in order to better understand what's gone awry in your relationship. Right now, you may not agree with everything you'll read below. But a few chapters down the pike, you will see precisely why I need you to entertain the possibility that some of what I suggest here may contain a few ounces of truth.

> **Men and women process sex and intimacy differently, yet each gender cannot accept that truth. We keep expecting our partners to perceive sex and intimacy as we do.**

Her Truth Isn't Your Truth
Once more, because I simply cannot state this too often, men and women process love, sex and intimacy (emotional closeness and physical "connectedness") *very differently*. Yet each gender cannot accept that truth, so both men and women persist in expecting their partners to perceive sex and experience it as *they* do. That's a major reason why many of us are in the messes we're in. (Of course, because male and female psyches alike contain both masculine and feminine elements, the "truths" in this chapter and in the next chapter about Female Truths may be more striking in some people and more subtle in others.)

But the point here is to understand ingrained male and female attitudes and behaviors ("truths") *as they actually exist*, not as you *assume* or *would like* them to be. If you can achieve this, your own actions regarding your relationship with your partner will be very different than they have been up to this point—*and much more productive!* You'll finally get a genuine start toward the sex life you want and, not coincidentally, so will your girl (even if, right now, she thinks no sex is the sex life she wants). In essence: *Know what you are doing and why you are doing it*, and you'll have greater control of your life and your pivotal love relationships. So, let's start with the male gender first:

Your 5 Truths
Following are five Male Truths that impact your long-term sexual relationship. Some may already be obvious to you, some you may take issue with, some may provoke thought. Many of these could be news to your wife/girlfriend/lover. But you will need to familiarize yourself with each of them—and then the Female Truths that follow—if you want to turn your sex life around.

> **To a man, sex IS love. Men need physical connectedness with a woman the way they need air to breathe.**

Truth No. 1: To a man, sex *is* love. Please understand: I am not saying that men fall in love with anyone who will sleep with them. What I am saying, however, is that sexual intimacy is generally how men know or perceive that *they are loved*. Men need physical connectedness with a woman the way they need air to breathe, water to drink, food to eat. In fact, if the male of the species were *not* endowed with this drive, then the species itself would not have survived—it would surely have died out while man was deciding if he was "in the mood" to procreate! Women may have a hard time accepting this truth about the basic male need for physical intimacy, but resisting reality seems as absurd to me as resisting the fact that the sky is blue. (Why isn't the sky pink? It's blue because it's *blue*, ladies. Deal with it.)

> A man won't believe a woman *genuinely* loves him—and won't feel a true love connection with her—if she does not have fairly regular sex with him. End of story.

Now, this does not mean that other things women do to make a man feel loved are not appreciated; they are. Most men do love it when women cook for them, make a lovely home for them, hug them, cuddle with them, go hiking/cycling/snorkeling with them—or any number of other things. But Truth No. 1 is this: A man will not believe that a woman *genuinely* loves him—and he will not feel a true love connection with his woman—if she does not have sex with him on some kind of regular basis. End of story.

Truth No. 2: Most men cannot deal with their woman's anger. The fact of the matter is: Women who are not getting enough attention from their husbands/boyfriends/lovers (and, as a result, are not sleeping with them) are often angry with their men. Furthermore, they either have not been able to express or resolve that anger, or else they have been *trying* to get their anger issues across to their mate and feel they are not being heard. Either way, the anger keeps ramping up. It's often the case that if a relationship is in a low-sex state, there's probably a pissed-off woman in the house *and* a man who:

a) **Would rather not face that fact.**
b) **Has faced the fact**, but doesn't believe he *deserves* his lady's anger.
c) **Has faced the fact**, but doesn't *know how* to deal with the anger (and thus, consequently, isn't).

The point is, not much sex (and, certainly, not much *good* sex) is taking place as a result, even if the man is trying to defuse that anger by buying gifts, doing chores, etc. An interesting note: A recently published (and unnamed here) self-help book advises women to "just do it," and get beyond the sexual stalemate so that both parties can start enjoying intimacy again. That solution may indeed get you one roll in the hay, even two. But sooner or later, your lady is going to have trouble stifling the anger that she cannot express outwardly, or that you are not willing or able to face. Then the sex will evaporate once again, and maybe for good.

All in all, it's far better to face the reality of Truth No. 2 right now, so that you can learn how to conquer it. And the best way to start learning to defuse your gal's anger, is to accept that the following Truths No. 3 and 4 are just...plain...true.

Truth No. 3: Men are 'magical' thinkers, when it comes to relationships. Most men are surprised, months or years into their relationship with their mate, at how fearless their woman is when it comes to attacking relationship problems. Sooner or later that fearlessness presents itself as an ability to zero-in on the offending challenge, confront it, draw it out, swing it around for all to see, jump on it to disable it entirely, and then attack it until it surrenders or expires, whichever comes first.

> **Men don't want problems rubbed in their faces—especially when those problems can go away 'magically.'**

Men are not at all like their women in this regard: If there's an obstruction lurking somewhere in the vicinity, a man is generally quite confident it will go away all by itself (magically!) so why get all *uncomfortable* about the thing? Simply put, men do not want problems rubbed in their faces. (There's only one thing men want rubbed, and it's never yet been a face.) Men are so into magical thinking, in fact, that they are often blissfully unaware that they even *have* a real problem on their hands—until it explodes.

Truth No. 4: When it comes to relationships, men often seem lazier than women. All right: If you were waiting for a Male Truth to take issue with, this may be the one. Then again, it may not. After all, even though you run a company, can work a backhoe, build whole bathrooms on weekends, and take out enough garbage annually to create a landfill, let's face it: You've always secretly suspected that you have a lazy streak. Maybe that's because, earlier on, your mother continually pestered you to do things that were designed to interfere with your television-watching, video game-playing, guitar strumming, or general shut-eye time, and you're concerned that the pattern may be repeating itself with your wife/girlfriend/lover.

Whether or not you believe you're doing your share (maybe even *more* than your share!) of the household duties, just how does male "laziness" help to perpetuate a low-sex relationship with a woman? Is this about agreeing to help with the dishes? Is this about getting the kids to their sports practices on the weekends?

> **Are men often guilty of a certain kind of laziness that has to do with attending to 'relationship stuff'?**

Or does Truth No. 4 have something to do with another kind of laziness altogether? Possibly a laziness about attending to "relationship stuff" that is just so darn annoying to deal with? Or maybe a reluctance to heed repeated signals or seriously deal with stated grievances? Hmmm...

Truth No. 5: Men cannot thrive without respect. I tried to think of many ways to identify this subheading. Among them were: Men Want Respect; Men Must Have Respect; Men Need Respect. But the truth of the matter is that men need respect in order to thrive or even *basically function* as psychologically healthy males. And it's not surprising that a man doesn't feel respected at all when his own wife or girlfriend won't sleep with him, particularly when she once seemed to love doing the deed with him.

Ironically, although I've listed this truth as Truth No. 5, the respect issue is frequently a major contributor to the low-sex relationship and often presents as a self-perpetuating situation that makes the low-sex cycle so hard to break (much more about this later). But with a little knowledge and practice, that cycle *can* be broken.

The curious thing—and the essential truth here—is that when it comes to respect issues, the change needed *doesn't* come first from the "non-respecter" (the female in the relationship). Bringing about change regarding respect will require the initiative of the individual who biologically, evolutionarily and psychologically needs to *lead* the sexual side of the man/woman relationship:

You.

Chapter 6
The Truth About Women

Now let's take a look at the six Female Truths. (Yes, women get more truths that men do. We're more complicated, but you knew that. Besides, women get extra everything, so why not truths?) These underlying truths may be much, much harder for you, a man, to accept. They may seem alien, unreasonable, or just downright insane. Yet if I am willing to reveal them to you (And why shouldn't I? After all, I *want* my own gender to find true happiness), then you'd do well to accept them, as is.

> **Commit to accepting that, with women, things are not as you *assumed* they were. And commit to accepting that things are definitely not as they are with men.**

Her 6 Truths
Again, the weight or dominance of each of these truths may vary in any given female individual. But to one degree or another, they exist in virtually all heterosexual women. The important thing to remember is that they all directly impact *your* sex life. Choose to say "No way! That can't be!" to any one of these truths, and you may never get back to where you dream of being with your mate. In other words: *Open your mind and commit to accepting that things are not as you assumed they were.* Open your mind and commit to accepting that things are *not* the same way that they are with YOU (a man).

Truth No. 1: Sex is not a primary need for many women; it is a *response*. It's pretty much just as you suspected: Most women in long-term relationships can live just fine without sex for much longer than you can. On the other hand, they can positively ache for it when you awaken real desire in them. They can even initiate sex (hooray!) when you are tuned in to the right ways to stimulate passion in them.

> Sex isn't a primary need for most women; it's a *response*. You've got to give your lady something she knows how to respond to!

The bottom line is: *You've got to give a woman something she knows how to respond to!* It turns out that women are great at responding, as long as you know how to press the correct buttons. They'll even out-and-out *tell you*, over and over again, which buttons you need to press! Ironically, though, many of those buttons have *little or nothing to do with* your sexual technique.

The problem is, when it comes to a man's drive toward sex, most men don't hear, believe or take much *non*-sexual information seriously. Men are much more physically and visually stimulated than women are and they don't believe that really good sex for women is ignited long before a physical interaction. Men do not believe that great sex can start with the female response to male behaviors and attitudes that precede any physical interaction at all. In other words, men simply do not believe that the sexual urge, for a woman, can arise from her *perception* of her male in totally *non*-sexual situations.

This is so important that I need to say it again: *Sexual desire for a woman starts with her response to male behaviors and attitudes that often come wayyy before any physical interaction.*

So, if (in your desperate search to find a solution to your low-sex relationship) you've been reading every sex book or blog about sexual foreplay technique that you can get your hands on, STOP RIGHT NOW!

> **For your woman, sexual response starts in the brain, not the groin.**

For women, sexual response starts in the *brain*, not in the groin. Only *then* does it move on to the hormonal systems that trigger desire. What's so frustrating is that many men say that they understand this, yet to rebuild their physical relationships with their women they continue to initiate with actions or words that are of a purely sexual nature. I understand: It's what you KNOW.

Then there are the more enlightened men who insist they approach sex with greater consideration: "It was Friday night and I brought her flowers and then took out the garbage without being asked. That way, I made it clear that I love her and care about her, before anything got sexual. But when I made my move, she *still* looked at me as though I were some kind of ogre. What gives?"

It may be difficult for you to accept this, but in an established relationship, a woman's desire response often is not stimulated by anything that a *man* would term sexual, romantic—or even considerate.

Don't believe me? Check out the following scenarios and note which ones have been getting you nowhere:

> ***Scenario One:*** It's a Sunday afternoon and the kids are out of the house (or you and your girlfriend find yourselves alone without company, work, errands, etc.). You put down the paper (or turn off the TV, put away the power drill) smile at her lustfully and ask, "Hey, wanna go in the bedroom?" (Or, "Wanna go lie down, get naked, take a shower?" etc., etc.) She ignores you or sighs and continues to read her fashion magazine, mumbling something about cramps.
>
> ***Scenario Two:*** Your wife (or girlfriend/lover) comes home from working (or you both finally get the kids to bed after a full

day). She scurries about to get dinner ready (you thoughtfully assure her you will be happy to clean up), and while she is slicing an onion at the counter and monitoring a pot of water boiling for macaroni, you slip behind her, grab her around her waist (or playfully honk "the girls") and let her know that you're thinking about her great body and that you'll be ready for friskiness whenever she is. But, "Honey! I'm trying to get *dinner* ready!" she protests. Then she suggests you make yourself useful by setting the table.

Scenario Three: You and your wife/girlfriend have a talk about your sexual stalemate and she reveals that she doesn't believe you find her attractive. You've insisted over and over again that you do (she's a woman, she's soft and cuddly, and you chose her above all others—of *course* she's attractive). But you now realize you need to do something more than just reassure her. So the next day when you pick her up at the gym, determined to woo her properly for a night of passion ahead, you make certain to greet her with "Hi Gorgeous!"—not minding at all that she's a bit greasy, her hair is unkempt and sticking to her face, and large perspiration stains are working their way down the center of her chest and underneath each armpit. She rolls her eyes at your greeting and, as soon as you both get home, she heads for the shower, making no effort to mask the sound of the bathroom door locking.

Scenario Four: You actually made it into bed together and enjoyed some form of sexual interlude. You appreciated every minute of it and are remembering that you should let her know that you think she's attractive, and you may not have been paying enough attention to this for the past days/weeks/months. So you make *sure* to tell her about the parts of her body that turn you on. (If that doesn't reassure her, what will?) "I wish you didn't only care about my body," she responds in curiously subdued tones, leaving you to ponder precisely what *that* meant.

If any of these four scenarios sound familiar, you do not "get" the concept that, for a woman, sexual desire is a *response*—a response to behaviors and actions that *mean* something to her, and which come *way before* sex is on the horizon.

> **Her sexual desire is a response to behaviors and actions that *mean* something to her, and come *way before* sex is on the horizon.**

Truth No. 2: Your woman needs to be *actively* loved and valued, if you want to have regular sex with her. This is probably the Truth that most men have the hardest time understanding and dealing with. And if you're saying to yourself, "What the hell does 'actively loved' or 'actively valued' mean?" then you're one of them. I'm going to devote a good deal of time to this in Part II, because Truth No. 2 is THAT important.

In the meantime, let me ask you this: How many times have you heard about or read about the breakup of a wealthy couple who seemingly had everything, and yet the wife filed for divorce with the complaint, "He gave me everything except himself"? Did you wonder what she meant by that? Did you mentally write it off as typical female whining, making no sense whatsoever? Has your wife or girlfriend ever said something like that to *you*?

If she has, or if she has ever complained that she's "lonely" or she "misses you," or you "never spend time together anymore" (especially when you work together every day or see each other's faces across the dining table every morning and evening), then Chapters 8 and 9, all about active loving, are designed for *you*.

> **A wealthy couple is divorcing because the wife claims, 'He gave me everything except himself'? Do you write off her complaint as typical female whining?**

And if you study those two chapters as though your life depends on it, you'll do more to revive your sex life (and a happy life, in general, with your partner) than by doing anything else.

In the meantime, don't panic. You won't have to buy matching cycling outfits or go to the mall every weekend. Learning how to give your beloved regular *authentic* (I don't like that word, but it actually works here) attention will not plunge you into the 24-hour-a-day "togetherness" hell most men fear and imagine. And, honestly, picking up these skills is not hard work; it's just a matter of knowing *how*.

Truth No. 3: A woman's love response is *directly proportionate to your value of her*. This is a tough female Truth to explain to any living man, because the male libido has little or no identification with this reality. And that's because while a man may be annoyed or even hurt that his woman appears not to value him as much as he feels she should—he'll still have sex with her any way he can get it.

A woman, however, is not built that way. She will quietly gauge her man's value of her in many ways—the consideration he shows her in public; how often he takes her to dinner, and where; how thoughtful his gifts to her are (and even how relatively frugal or generous); how he speaks about her to others; how much time he is willing to take away from others, to give to her; and so on and so forth.

And she will feel only as loved as the value she determines he places on her.

"Ah hah!" you are saying, "I *knew* this was all about money, gifts, houses, and furs!" Well hold on there, mister, because here's where the confusing part comes in: Your girl doesn't necessarily want whatever is *costly*. All she wants to know is that she is worth something that represents some value and sacrifice to *you*. Let me put it this way:

Scenario One: Sheila and her husband have been married for 15 years. This year for her 40th birthday, he bought her a shiny new sedan he had been talking about, yet she feels as though she doesn't mean very much to him. In light of such a sizable investment, how can that possibly be? "I was hoping for a sentimental jewelry gift," she laments, thinking of the lovely necklace they had discovered together on a recent trip. But her husband had made it fairly clear that he didn't see the point in "frivolous" expenditures, when for the same amount of money they could have a good, solid car for the family. Sheila, though, is already wondering how she can avoid telling her friends about her 40th birthday gift. She imagines the look of pity on their faces as they whisper that her husband doesn't love her anymore.

Scenario Two: Katy is married to a man who, for her birthday, did not purchase a gift for her. Instead, Katy woke up on her birthday morning to see him standing by her bedside with a bed tray. On it was a plate of scrambled eggs, toast, coffee, and a rose from their yard, tucked into a waterless bud vase.

Katy grinned with delight as she spied her husband by her side. He'd been invited to go to the playoffs with friends, but he didn't go, and was happy not to. He wanted to stay home to cook his wife her birthday breakfast.

On this morning, he rose early to take the kids to their grandmother's house and then hurry back home to wake his wife with love. "Today, it's all about you" he announced to Katy, and then detailed a day devoted to her favorite pastimes—window shopping, lunch in the park, and a back- and foot-rub from him, topped off by a classic movie marathon at home with take-out Chinese. "We may not have much of a bank balance in this crummy economy," he told her gently, "but there's nothing I wouldn't do to make you happy." Katy hugged him for all she was worth because she knows she married a man who would indeed do whatever he possibly could to give her a wonderful birthday. Katy feels more than loved; she feels cherished and adored.

Do you value *your* woman enough to give up playoff tickets? Part with money you would rather have spent on something you wanted for yourself? Buy her something she would adore even if *you* don't see the value in it? Put a down payment on a vacation or an eternity ring—even if you'd rather sleep on the cash? Take her dancing, shopping, to the ballet—even if you *hate* those things? Spend time with her even when you believe she'll be just fine while you have fun elsewhere?

> **How much is she worth to you? Women wear their men's value of them like badges for the world to see. *Your* woman may be wishing you valued her more than you do.**

Just how much is your woman worth to you? Men don't know this but, just as *they* drive hot cars to show the world they have "arrived," *women* wear their husbands' value of them like badges for all the world (read: other *women*) to see. So you'd better carefully examine the issue of your woman's worth, because your lady is getting your message louder and more clearly than you'd ever imagine. And while some women can *appear* to be quite forbearing, sooner or later the hurts will pop out just when you least expect them.

If, by your own "reasonable" standards, you're still convinced that you've always done enough, I beg you to stop here for a moment and try to honestly reassess things from *her* standpoint. Never forget that your woman is gauging things by her *own* standards, and she may already be having a great deal of trouble forgiving you for not placing a higher value on her presence in your life. If you think about it, many of her hurts or disappointments may have already been rearing their ugly little heads each time you were hoping she'd jump passionately into bed with you.

> **If your other voice says, 'I'm sure she'll think this last-minute gift is okay; she's pretty understanding,' stop in your tracks! It's *not* okay and she will *not* think it is.**

Here's a little reality check for you to use: Let's say you are preparing to grab that slap-dash last-minute birthday gift for her, or explain to her that you can't accompany her to a friend's party because the game is on. Then, out of nowhere, your "other" voice whispers to you, "Will she think this is okay? Yah—I'm sure she'll think it's okay. She's always pretty understanding." Warning!! If you hear that voice, *stop in your tracks and immediately accept the following:* It's *not* okay, and she will *not* think it is okay. She will, however, decide that you don't value her very much anymore. With a woman, it's Pay Me Now or Pay Me Later. So...

Make the extra effort to let her know you value her. Do not take her for granted! Make a smaller sacrifice *up front* (a gift with meaning for her; attending a party of her friends), instead of unwittingly sacrificing your own sex life with the woman you love.

Truth No. 4: Women must feel beautiful, to feel desirable. Again, I tried to think of many ways to identify this subheading, for we all know that not every woman can be a supermodel. That doesn't matter. Not every *man* can be a pulsating, virile stud either, but that doesn't mean that *you* don't want to feel like one and, at critical moments, believe that your woman sees you this way, too.

Still, even if you believe this particular Female Truth is silliness, I am revealing to you perhaps the greatest secret you will ever discover about women: Women *must* feel beautiful—and must believe that you see them as beautiful—in order to function well sexually. It is astounding to me how few men take this truth seriously, or else are convinced that a "Hey you like nice tonight" every month or two, will suffice.

> **Your woman *must* feel beautiful—and must believe that you see her as beautiful—in order to function well sexually.**

Then again, you may have thought that getting your woman into bed had everything to do with *you* looking good to *her*. (There is of course a certain amount of truth in that: We certainly do not want to sleep with reeking oafs who don't give a hoot about hygiene.) But the crux of the matter is that while you may have thought your sexual success with her was all about *you*, it's really all about *her* (what a surprise). To state it plainly: A woman won't happily sleep with her man unless *she* feels sexy and desirable. And a woman doesn't feel genuinely desirable unless she is convinced that her man believes she is beautiful. Truly beautiful. More beautiful than any other woman he knows or ever will know. On any planet. Forever.

Yes, we are that insecure. But if you are having trouble accepting this female fact of life, then think about it in a way that you may be able relate to: Our beauty is to us what your penis is to you—the most vulnerable thing we've ever brought into a bed. You may worry about size, performance, how well endowed her last boyfriend was. We wonder if you think we are anywhere near as pretty and charming as the girl who smiled at you in the restaurant—or if you're just in bed with us for the sex. Are we clear?

The most amazing aspect of this Truth is that, in their private lives, even movie stars and sex goddesses have admitted they don't believe that they are beautiful (without their makeup and styling teams). At least, not unless their men tell them that they are, and *why* they are, and so make them believe it, too.

Now that you know this, is it so surprising that a woman who doesn't feel beautiful does not feel sexually desirable and thus *may not want to engage in sex or be able to feel desire for YOU?* Remember: Because men and women have such different needs when it comes to sex, you must be careful about projecting your feelings about *yourself* into this scenario: While you may be able to function sexually even if your bedmate thinks you look like a troll, a woman simply cannot!

> **Evolutionarily, her sense of her beauty and your sex life are linked: Women survived only if they were *attractive* enough to mate with, gather food for, and keep from harm.**

Not surprisingly, it may all hearken back to evolution and the survival of the fittest: The most capable, virile men survived because they could protect themselves and their families, gather food, kill predators, and procreate. (Note that there is no mention here about what they actually *looked* like.) Likewise, the most *desirable* (read: beautiful, feminine, alluring) *women* survived because they could attract men to mate with them, gather food for them, make babies with them, and keep them from harm.

Still dubious? Try this little experiment: Just before you put the moves on your lady, mention with concern that she looks tired. Or, better yet, remark that the girl in the movie you both just watched was indeed stunning. Then see how far you get. (You've already been there and done that? Oh you poor clueless man!)

Truth No. 5. Women *want* to respect men; they *want* them to keep their power. Okay, she's angry and in a hundred different ways she's letting you know it. One of those ways is that she's not sleeping with you. But, just as serious, she's not respecting you, either. She used to adore everything you did, every move you made, every clever word that came out of your mouth. Now you can't even open a jar properly. Am I right? And (if you haven't already given up trying to please her) you're jumping around like a marionette, trying to keep her happy and hoping to keep that razor-sharp tongue from lashing you to bits.

Not a pretty picture. In fact, life with your darling girl is *so* uncomfortable these days, you wonder why you even *want* to sleep with her. But alas, sex is like air, food and water to you. It's a direct route to feeling loved and valued, and you'd do just about anything to keep the hope alive.

Yet, here's the irony of it all: The more you allow her to disrespect you, and the more you allow her to erode your power, the more she will hate herself for doing it and will hate *you* for allowing her to do it! Worse, the less she will want to sleep with you.

> **The more you allow her to disrespect you, the more she'll hate herself for doing it and *you* for allowing her to! She wants a man who would never let her behave so badly.**

No matter what she says, she does *not* want a yes-man.

Sure, she needs you to pitch in with her; she wants you to let her know that you're happy to help carry the load in life and don't want to grind her into the ground with drudgery. But she did not marry you to keep her kitchen floor scuff-mark clean. Yes, she needs help and consideration where any human being would be kind and thoughtful, but she doesn't want household or other assistance at the expense of losing the happy, confident man she fell in love with.

> **She wants *you*, with your power intact, the way you were before you allowed her anger to unravel you.**

Furthermore, if you have given up your power, she is *furious* that she can no longer bask in the glow of your self-respect as she parades you proudly around town. She's longing for the return of the man who respects himself as much as he respects her. She wants back the man who would never tolerate her behaving so badly. She wants the man who would *never* be afraid of her and her moods. (And you *are* just a little afraid of her, aren't you?)

She wants *you*, with your power intact, the way you were before you allowed her anger to unravel you.

The fact of the matter is, she will put up with any number of (nonintentional) household mishaps and other human missteps and never raise that dreaded eyebrow, if you will just stop being afraid of her and treat her lovingly and considerately *but without sacrificing yourself in the process*.

This Truth—the uncomfortable truth about your loss of self-respect—may be hard to swallow, but it's a necessary first step if your woman is to see you with new desiring eyes. And it's never too late: Even if you can acknowledge that in some ways you have allowed yourself to become terribly diminished by your mate, recovery *is* achievable.

Now for the final Truth about women:

Truth No. 6. For *passionate* sex, a woman needs to be properly pursued and seduced. Do you know how to pursue and seduce your sweetheart? Do you—like millions of love-starved men around the world—think that being in a relationship means you no longer *need* to do these things? Do you simply *ask* her for sex or (God help you) let her know you *expect* it? Take a look at the following definitions:

- **Ask:** To call on for an answer; to make a request of.
- **Expect:** To regard as likely to happen.
- **Seduce:** To persuade; to lead away; to lead astray by persuasion; to entice to sexual intercourse; to attract.

Now that you've had a moment to consider the actual definitions of these three words: *ask, expect,* and *seduce*—which of the three makes you feel more manly? (Hint: The one that makes you *feel* more manly, will also make you more masculine in your woman's eyes, and masculinity sends female hormones zinging.)

Now put yourself in your lady's place for a moment: Which of these actions—to *ask, expect* or *seduce*—do you suspect might make *her* feel more desirable and thus more beautiful? (Hint: Never forget Truth No. 2—A woman who feels beautiful feels sexual.)

In case you're having a bit of trouble accepting the information above, I'm going to give it to you right between the eyes: If you don't know how to properly pursue and then seduce your mate, if you are unwilling to learn or relearn the art of seduction, or if you've decided you shouldn't *have* to seduce your own wife or longtime girlfriend anymore, then you do not care about seeming your most masculine to her; you do not care about making her feel most beautiful and womanly; and you will continue to sleep alone without a soft, lovely female who is happy to make you feel like a man.

> **Don't ask for sex from your lover the way you might request eggs for breakfast. *Seduce her* and get back to your animal origins!**

And in case you misguidedly believe that asking her permission for sex ("Hey, wanna go into the bedroom?") is the way to go, I say this to you: It matters not if men's magazines, advice books or blogs have told you that you must be "considerate" of your partner—*Don't ask for sex from your lover the way you might request eggs for breakfast!*

Being a considerate lover means: I give to you, you give to me; I consider your needs, you consider mine. But "considerate" does *not* mean asking for sex. Sex does not announce itself on your daily roster of requests and activities, and it's not about front-parlor etiquette. Sex is the lusty, magnificent, spontaneous expression of our animal origins and if you treat it as less than that, you'll *get* less than that—much less. Don't you want to get back to those glorious origins?

As for "expecting" sex from your lady because she has committed to loving you, that's just about as misguided as "expecting" a fully home-cooked dinner every night for the rest of your life, because you've put a ring on her finger.

> **Her sex-charging hormones don't pump as they should without some kind of *pre*-sexual 'mating dance'—even if that dance is only three minutes of trying to make her laugh.**

The truth is (and maybe this hearkens back to biological processes and evolution), a female intuitively expects a man to *vie* for her physical attention, at least on some level, even if it amounts to three minutes of trying to charm her or make her laugh before things move on to another stage. The feminine sex-charging hormones simply don't pump as they should without some kind of *pre*-sexual "mating dance"—and maybe this is what they mean when they say that the seduction of a woman takes place between her ears, not between her legs.

Unlike men, our juices don't start flowing when the mere prospect of sex is in the air, or when a genital is grabbed. Sadly, too, the knowledge that you helped subsidize a home some years ago or bought flowers for us on Tuesday doesn't secure you a romp this Saturday evening, either.

So, if your sex life has fallen by the wayside, some of that unhappy circumstance may have everything to do with the fact that you have taken to asking for sex or else expecting it as your due. You can do that all you want, but if what you *really* want is great sex, more frequent sex, even mind-bending sex with someone you love, then always remember the first three words below, and never forget them:

> **Sex is primal. Some bit of stalking needs to be involved when your Bambi trots by and looks mighty good to you. Or she'll trot on.**

Sex Is Primal

There's just no way around this one, and I'm afraid you *will* have to get off the darn couch if you want the sex life of your dreams. Some bit of stalking (pursuing) and mating-dancing (seduction) needs to be involved each time your Bambi trots by and looks mighty good to you, or she'll just trot on by. If you don't know how to seduce your lady love, you'll learn (or re-learn) the basics in Part II, coming up right now.

Part II – Change That, Fast

Chapter 7
Fanning Her Flames of Sexual Response

Remember the first of the Male and Female Truths? They stated that, for men, sex is the way men feel loved; sex is as essential as air, water and food. But for women, sex is more of a *response* than it is a primary need. In past decades, so much has been written, explaining that women don't necessarily respond to the same types of things that initially arouse men: sexual or visual stimuli, for instance. But have you ever accepted the idea that the female sexual "response" is precisely that—not as much a primary need as it is a response to YOU?

Now don't get me wrong: In the initial stages of dating, serious dating and lovemaking, it takes next to nothing to get two hormonally charged lovers to rush to a bed (or anything else close enough to make love on). The sight of a naked man (hell, the sight of a *man*) can be enough to get any woman caught up in the throes of lust, at that juncture.

> The 'art' of lovemaking is about keeping sex alive and kicking in the real world of jobs, children, finances and other stresses.

But we're not talking about those days; were talking about *these* days—your life in an established relationship—and these days are different. In actuality, it is in the long-term established relationship where the true "art" of lovemaking comes in: a term that surely wasn't coined for young, sweaty, undulating bodies that, in their first exposures to each other, gave less of a darn about "art" than about biology.

The true art of lovemaking is all about keeping sex alive and kicking in the *real* world, when sweethearts have made lives and families together, and when finances, jobs, disappointments and stresses—and everything in between—have intervened, doing a great good job of obscuring two rabid young lovers who have kept trying to get back to one another across the years.

Happily, you, the man in this story, will nurse your primary sex drive all the way to your grave, eternally hunting for a warm body with breasts and thighs and lovely secret parts. If it weren't for you, dear sir, sex as we know it might have become archaic eons ago. All *you* need is a glimpse of cleavage to fire things up again.

But for women—who must wear so many different hats daily and be so many things to so many different people—it often takes more than a random penis sighting or your reference to our breasts, to yank us back from the reality of daily life (kids, work, house, etc.), and rekindle *our* fires.

Women are Strange Creatures Indeed

What turns women on can be so alien to men! Is it any wonder you have trouble accepting that our triggers are the momentous things they are, to us. But though they are alien to you, those turn-ons can be many, and it would serve you so well to take them seriously!

> **A woman's turn-on can be as simple as a look across a room, or a gesture made in public that tells others you prize her.**

Our turn-on could be as simple as a look from you, across a room, or even your passing (non-sexual) touch. It could be any of the following, for instance: A gesture made in public that tells others you prize us. The lowering of your voice. A sudden, genuine expression of admiration from you. Your reaction of protection in a circumstance threatening to us. Your sudden expression of interest or concern, where none existed moments before. The way you look and smell, right out of the shower. The way you good-naturedly handle an emergency, or swoop in to relieve us of the kids. The "civilizing" of your masculinity in a well-tailored suit and crisp white shirt and tie. Your newfound interest in wearing good cologne to bed and watching a favorite movie with us. Your need to stand up for your rights, even if it means standing up to *us*. Your sense of conviction in the face of great odds. The way you describe, in unique detail, what you love about us, or about the way we look. The way you put your arm around us, to keep the world's harm at bay (or to let the world know that we are yours, and you are so proud of that). A sudden moment of self-revelation that you share with us. The way you love our faces as much as you love our bodies, even though there's no sexual gratification in that for you.

The lesson here? To understand what ignites your sweetheart's sexual response—

Remember the Other Male and Female Truths!
Understand that the Male and Female Truths that are not turn-*offs* (like asking for sex—remember that one?) are behind the Great Turn-*ons*. They're not just something we women like or something interesting about how we perceive our men: They are your dyed-in-the-wool, genuine First Steps to Sex.

Chapter 8
Magical Thinking vs.
Active Loving and Valuing

So much of Magical Thinking (Male Truth No. 3) seems to hook right up to our Female Truths Nos. 2 and 3: Your woman needs to be *actively* loved and valued, if you want to have regular sex with her. Magical Thinking gets right in the way of that.

The truth is that men in relationships don't always grasp their woman's intense need to be *actively* loved first, and somewhat regularly, before being approached for sex. Men are just too good at Magical Thinking ("Hmmm, I wonder what's bothering her? I'm sure if I just leave her alone or go off to work, it'll take care of itself..."). And unfortunately, they tend to use Magical Thinking a LOT when it comes to their lapses in the active loving and valuing department. Maybe it's part and parcel of relationship "laziness" (Male Truth No. 4); or maybe it's just the way the male mind works (ever hopeful)—who knows?

Take Mike and Anna, for example. Mike and Anna were both personal trainers for the same fitness company before two children came along in rapid succession. But the couple decided that Anna would be the home-based parent until the kids were in grade school and, during that time, Mike would shoulder the family's financial support.

Before their son and daughter were born, Mike and Anna not only spent a good deal of time working together, exercising together, and sharing new fitness techniques with each other, they frequently met for lunch and dinner during the week, as well. Their leisure weekend activities generally revolved around sports: bicycling, running, watching each other's weekend league sport activities. You might say it was hard to find two people so engaged in each other and in activities they both loved. They were *so* connected, in fact, that sex was generally spontaneous and instinctive: a glance, a laugh, a shared reference and before they knew it, they were in bed, on the carpet, or sneaking a roll on a grassy knoll somewhere.

Since the family transition three years ago, however, things have changed. Anna is wrapped up in the kids at home, while Mike is still going like gangbusters at the fitness studio and with his sports activities on most weekends. Anna and the kids tag along on those weekends, whenever possible.

Yet, Anna admits, "Even though I've got my kids with me all day—and I love them dearly—I'm really lonely for all the time Mike and I used to spend together. These days, when Mike gets home, things are pretty chaotic and we don't have time to ourselves until the kids go off to bed—and not even then, sometimes."

Mike, however, still looks for fairly regular sex, Anna reports. "And I really *do* want to have that kind of time alone with him," she insists, "but I can't turn it on and off that easily, when I feel so cut off from him. I need some love first!"

Her husband is bewildered when he hears this kind of statement from his wife, for he's always told her that he loves her, and she certainly must know that he does. Yet he's been getting a lot of such "complaints" from her lately.

"I just don't understand her," he confides. "I *finally* get home and we *finally* have time alone together, which I've been dying for. She says she misses me too, but the minute I suggest we hit the sheets and go for some serious lovemaking, she says that she just wants to know that I love her first. *Love* her? I'm waiting all day to get home to her!"

'Actively' Love Her Back Into Bed

The scenario above is a great example of neither party being "wrong" or "right." It's about how people *perceive* being loved. Simply put: While, to a man, being deeply loved is tied up in the physical (sexual) demonstration of love (among other things, of course), to a woman, love means different types of actions and behaviors, as well—and, usually, *first*. (To her, love is not just about *saying* that you love her and assuming that the knowledge is magically banked somewhere, for withdrawals as needed!)

Importantly, without her own special kinds of love *actions* from you, your girl does not have the triggers or cues that she needs to start her hormones firing up toward sex.

> **Without her own special kinds of love actions from you, your girl doesn't have the triggers she needs to fire up her sex hormones.**

So, in Mike and Anna's scenario above, all that's really happened is that while Mike still gets the same "cues" that have always led *him* into sex, Anna is now minus *her* love cues, and thus is having trouble responding to Mike, which is confounding and frustrating both of them. Mike's cues were, and still are, all of those below.

His Cues:

- **The visual stimulus** of seeing his love object naked, dressing or (especially!) undressing.
- **Caring actions from his love object**, such as greeting him happily at the door, making him dinner, asking him how his day was, etc., etc.
- **Missing his love object** while he is at work and she is at home with the kids.
- **Fantasizing about his love object** while he is at work and she is at home with the kids.
- **Noticing another female**, which reminds him of his own mate, waiting at home.

- Thinking about sex.
- Thinking about sex.
- Thinking about…well, you get the idea.

This is not to say that Mike doesn't have moments when his wife's glance or her laughter or their alone time together turns him on. After all, Mike is not a sperm machine; he's a human being! But, as a man, his primary turn-ons probably do tend more toward stimuli that are visual and imaginative.

> **There are so many 'alien' female turn-ons, it would take more pages than this one, to try and list them all!**

Anna's primary cues toward sex are different, and have more to do with feeling "actively" loved and valued by Mike, than with glimpsing his butt as he undresses for bed. Anna's cues more likely encompass those below.

Her Cues:
- **Getting sincere and interested attention** from him.
- **Having time alone with him to talk**, dream, laugh, share.
- **Having time alone with him to wander**, shop, see a movie, go out to dinner, sight-see, partake in sports, etc.
- **Getting spontaneous and heartfelt affection** (*non*-sexually first, is most convincing).
- **Being the recipient of his loving thoughts** about her, **or his valuing actions** toward her.
- **Being indulged by him**, with no ulterior motive in sight, but just because she means so much to him; he values her so highly. (And yes—this *could* mean a little spontaneous gift here or there for, to a woman, a gift combines attention, valuing and indulgence—the trifecta!—as long as it's not a *substitute* for authentic attention and affection.)

- **Being charmed by him.**
- **Being pursued by him.**
- **Being made to feel beautiful** and thus womanly and desired by him.
- **Being the object of his earnest seduction** efforts to "win" her (because he values her sexual and love attentions so very highly).

Do these cues seem alien to you? The truth is that there are so many more "alien" female turn-ons (e.g., seeing her man dressed up for her; watching him make a fool of himself for her) that it would take more pages than this one, to try to list them all!

> **Men have a tough time understanding how *indirect* things could be sexual turn-ons.**

Here again, men have a tough time understanding how such *indirect* things could be sexual turn-ons, when their own triggers are so much more straightforward, logical and physical. Don't women *ever* think and feel about things as a man does?

The answer is: Of course! Certainly, your sweetheart misses you! Naturally, she appreciates your body and can be stirred by it. Sure, she has the knowledge that you love her. And I guarantee you that she still wants to connect with you physically. *She just can't always get there the way that you do*, and if you keep believing that she eventually will, or should, or could if only she really wanted to (or if only you leave the whole thing alone for a week, month or year), you'll just go around and around inside your bubble of Magical Thinking forever while your most important life relationship erodes.

And all this, ironically, while the two of you are actually trying to find your way back to each other, yet getting more hurt and disappointed with each setback. Wouldn't it be easier to simply learn how to practice the active loving and valuing cues that will lead her back to bed (and deepen your relationship in the process)?

> **You already know how to give her the 'cues' she needs to get back to bed: You gave them to her *instinctively*, when you were dating!**

The amazing thing is—as we discussed in the beginning of this book—you actually *already* know how to do all of these things: You did them *instinctively* when you were dating her! And you don't even have to do them on the same level that you did them then (although I am convinced that there is indeed a direct correlation between the quality and frequency of your active loving and valuing, and the quality and frequency of the resulting sex). But you *do* have to get back into "active" mode (and out of Magical Thinking mode) if you want any kind of sex life.

The reality is that, as a man, *your* part of the magic equation (how to actively love and value your woman the way she needs it) usually leads to *her* part of the magic equation (sleeping with you enthusiastically). And, as you've no doubt discovered, the reverse is unfortunately true, as well: Screw up your end of the equation and, sooner or later, the sex just stops coming.

> ***Your* part of the magic equation (love us the way we need it) leads to *our* part of the equation (sleeping with you enthusiastically). Screw up your end and sex stops coming.**

Now that I've said this, I can almost hear the wheels turning inside your sex-starved brain: *It's just sex! Why is this such a big deal? Am I going to have to hold her hand and go shopping with her forever, just to get a decent boink from the woman who is supposed to love me?*

The answer is No. It's all about a change of *attitude*. It's amazing how a little enlightenment goes a long, long way and affects your daily behavior even when you are unaware of it. And once your sweetheart feels that you "get" her, there will be many times that YOU will get it when you weren't even going for it. (Get it?)

Coming From Opposite Sides of Sex and Love
When a man has sex, he feels loved.
When a woman feels loved, she feels sexual.

> **When a man has sex, he feels loved.**
> **When a woman feels loved, she feels sexual.**

This difference between men and women is critical to you rediscovering a healthy sex life with your lady love. And if it sounds to you as though men and women were created to start out on opposite sides of the bed, you're right; they were. But what does it matter, *as long as they meet in the middle*—right in the center of that bed, in a steamy embrace and whatever comes next?

The difficulty, as many women see it, is that they are too often expected to approach sex and love in the style of men—sex first. And while most women have no problem with that approach now and again, they get frustrated, then hurt, then resentful (yes, we get darn resentful!) when sex is too infrequently approached in the way that works best for a *woman*: some active love and attention *first*.

> **You keep wanting her to approach sex in the way that works best for *you*: sex first, closeness after. You've forgotten to do it her way, too: Closeness first, sex resulting.**

Now, most women have, at one time or another, tried to tell their man that he needs to stop being obtuse and take note of this difference, if everyone wants to be happy. Most men have actually received this kind of request from their woman, couched in various ways. Yet many have never *heard* it. Not so much because they don't care about the issue; and certainly not because they don't want to understand what's going wrong. As I've said, most men insist they would do *anything*, if only their gals would want to make love to them more often.

The problem is that men just don't "get" that their women need some special, non-sexual closeness first, before sex is even on the horizon, so that their sexual feelings for their men can become aroused.

Why Don't Men 'Get It'?
There are a number of possible reasons why they don't:

- **First, men often cannot translate female complaints** that are not posed in a straightforward manner. In female-ese, "We don't spend enough time together anymore" means just that, but it also means: "You want me to sleep with you on demand, but can't I have a little of your time and attention first, and some kind of connecting prior to the event, like we used to have?" (For decades now, men have been informed that women do not "heat up" as fast as men do, but what they do not grasp is that the "heating up" period needs to begin way before sexual foreplay; it begins with *non*-sexual attention, *first*.)

- **Second, men frequently 'tune out'** even when the issue *is* presented to them, directly. That's because, to a man, a direct statement asking for more time together may immediately be perceived as an *accusation* designed to expose inadequacy: In male-ese, her statement, "I need to spend more time with you" doesn't mean, "I love you and want to see more of you," or even, "If you would just spend a little more time with me, I would feel so much sexier and eager to engage..." In male-ese it means: "You asshole. You're a lousy [husband or boyfriend] and you don't know the first thing about how to be a good one." Yet, to a woman, that interpretation is insane! To a man, however, the interpretation is justified: It reflects everything that rushes to his surface when his woman even *sounds* like she is complaining about a creeping lack of attention.

> **If you haven't accepted her problem, it's because you don't understand female-ese. You're hearing the information as whining, complaining, accusing and ego-bashing.**

- **Third, instructions may be forthcoming.** A man can "tune out" even when, in an honest and direct fashion, his woman is *trying to help him understand* the differences between them ("Honey, can we please sit down and have a talk about the best ways to help our sex life?"). It may be an old joke that men will do almost anything to avoid having to follow explicit (toy assembly/freeway/garbage disposal) directions, but a woman will tell you that the minute her voice takes on the tone of "Directions Will Follow," her man's eyes actually do glaze over. And we haven't even touched on the *panic* that engulfs him the minute he hears the words "...help our sex life," once again indicating that he alone is failing, failing, failing at something his male peers in the universe are handling just fine.

For so many reasons, men keep getting blocked from hearing what their women are so desperately trying to tell them. And women become frustrated and hurt when their man (who professes to love them) would rather do anything than hear about what small adjustments may be needed to bring two people joyfully to the center of their bed.

I suspect that in addition to all of the obstructions discussed above (or maybe *contributing* to them), there may also be other culprits, such as:

- **A man's legitimate difficulty comprehending** what is being asked of him, even if he hears it. "Time together," for instance, can be so vague and huge-sounding to a man. What exactly does "time together" refer to? Time doing what? And how *much* time? How can he gauge it?

- **A man's deep-seated fear** that his woman's unmet need is too complicated, mysterious, or abstract for him to meet—and his fear that both of them will soon know he can't measure up.

> **Be honest and ask yourself this: Has she been *trying* to tell you what's wrong? Have you simply decided that her alien 'female' requests are not worth taking seriously?**

Worse Than Not 'Getting It'

There's one more gremlin, though; one more possible reason why a man is not hearing his woman even after hints, attempts at humor, little complaints, big complaints, "heart-to-heart" talks, or out-and-out battles. The gremlin is this:

He believes that her requests to better "connect" prior to sex are trivial, unimportant, ridiculous or, for whatever reason, not to be taken very seriously. Yet to imagine how your partner must feel if you believe her need for non-sexual attention prior to sex is just silliness, ask yourself this:

Are *you* happy when she sees your own (verbal or other) requests for *sexual* attention as ridiculous or unimportant?

Admit it: Without sex, you are as good as unloved. Well, as far as she's concerned, without some *non*-sex-related love and attention beforehand, she just can't get warmed up for sex! That's not her decision to be contrary and cause you unhappiness; that's the way she's *made*, brother.

> **Without sex, you feel as good as unloved. (That's how you're *built*.) Well, without closeness and attention first, she can't get warmed up for sex. (That's how *she's* built.)**

Given the actual state of affairs and the way your mate is emotionally and hormonally constructed, wouldn't you prefer to leave magical thinking aside just long enough to get this "active loving and valuing" thing right so that after wonderful sex, you *both* feel happy, satisfied and fully loved? So that you *both* feel like you are magnificently fulfilling your partner's most basic human needs? Of course you do, or you wouldn't have paid darn good money for this book.

Chapter 9
How to Actively Love and Value

It's Saturday night. You've spent the whole wonderful day together and now the two of you have rushed home to get ready for an evening out. She emerges from the bedroom wearing a fabulous dress, looking gorgeous and sexy and, suddenly, you know you've got to have her. You sidle up to her and wind your big, strong arms around her in a way that thrills her and makes her feel beautiful and desirable. In fact, you whisper huskily that she *is* beautiful...

OR, is the following scenario closer to your reality these days?

It's Saturday night and though you and she have passed like ships in the night for the past week, hey, it's *Saturday night*. You're thinking: *We haven't had time together in a week; we've barely even had two minutes alone. This is gonna be great. We'll have a quick dinner, then some rip-roaring sex, and then we can lie around afterward and relax together.* (Sex first; then you'll feel connected and loved, right?)

So, as she stands at the stove in her sweats (yup; the kitchen analogy again), trying to get dinner on the table, you playfully make a grab for her backside or else suggest, "Hey, let's get into bed early tonight and have a little 'quality' time together, huh? Whatdya think, babe?"

She flashes you a look of weary tolerance. And she's thinking: *He hasn't said two words to me in a whole week! He doesn't even want to spend time with me or "be" with me! He doesn't love me anymore; he only wants me for sex.*

And she's thinking that because, as we've explained, she's eternally insecure about her desirability *as a woman* (which is different than being available for sex) and also because, in an established relationship, she needs your human (non-sexual) attention first, so that she feels noticed, valued, desired and, *thus*, sexual.

Hogwash, you say, and in your best Magical Thinking mode, you tell yourself that she probably was just focused on getting dinner on the table instead of jumping into bed with you right now and letting everything get cold. After all, it's only a *man* who would happily see a bowl of soup congeal, to be in the arms of his sweetheart.

> A man doesn't just want a woman to sleep with him; he wants a woman who *wants* to sleep with him. News Flash: Most women *want* to want their man that badly.

And that makes you a little sad because, more than anything (says a very smart man I know) a man wants a woman who *wants* to sleep with him; *wants* to share herself with him; *wants* to share her private and secret places with him. *Wants* him to make love to her. Even *demands* that he does!

Women *Want* to Want Their Men

Well, you may or may not believe this, but most women *do* want to be swept away by their man and find themselves lost in their lover's arms, his lust, his soul. Most women *do* want to want their men that badly!

You can help to make this happen by always remembering women need to feel actively loved and valued by you *before* you decide to approach them sexually. "Attention First" is a motto you'll have to adopt if you want to have cold soup and a hot, hot bed.

All right, you say: "You've made it abundantly clear that 'surfacing' on Friday night after a week under the water of my other concerns and interests, makes my mate feel as though I'm not even noticing her—let alone connecting or engaging with her—until I suddenly realize that the weekend has arrived and we have some 'together' time which, for me, means time in bed with her. I can see that I need to pay more regular attention to someone I expect will share physical love with me. I know this sounds ridiculous, but aside from stashing my smartphone and flipping off the football game, *what precisely do I do?*"

Your Ideal 'Love First' Scenario
Your goal now is to try to work your way at least *part* of the way back to those days of yore when you only had eyes for her, and all the time in the world to talk with her, laugh with her, share with her, gaze at her—and then make love to her. It was instinctive then, because you wanted her so badly. The bottom line: You'll need to land somewhere between the days when she had *all* of your attention, connection and engagement, and now, when she has so much less of it.

Start By Putting Aside Regular Time *Each Day*
—Even if it's a heartfelt 30 minutes (and I hope it's more). Dedicate that time to her, and to her alone. Then, make that time really *count*: Hold her hand when you walk together. Sit across from her at the hamburger joint and talk to her about your latest hopes and dreams (and make sure to ask her about hers). Look into her eyes and see again—for the first time in a long time—the little flickers of color you haven't noticed for so long. Watch her laugh, and appreciate again what a beautiful smile she has (or what lovely hair, or how wonderful she looks after all these years, or how charming that little dimple in her chin is). Perhaps it was the first thing you ever noticed about her. Above all else,

Make Sure You Tell Her About It!
Because if you don't *verbalize* what you think and feel, nothing has changed, as far as your lady is concerned.

The fact is: Women are verbal. Again, the old adage about is true:

For a woman, foreplay happens between the ears, not between the legs. So *tell* her what you love about how she looks. Make it *specific*, and keep it *non*-sexual (at least at first) or she will be convinced that you are thinking only about bed—which may be true, but for goodness' sake, make this about what *she* wants (to be loved, valued and admired), not about what *you* want (immediate carnal knowledge, you animal). She needs (just a little!) time, attention and words, to get her hormones pumping.

> **For a woman, foreplay really *does* happen between the ears, not the legs. She needs (just a little!) time, attention and words to get her hormones pumping.**

And yes, decoding female-ese can be tricky. Below are examples of what I mean by making it about what *she* wants (your admiration, love and high regard of her), and not what *you* want (sex):

DON'T say: "Mmmm, your skin feels great," as you stroke it. Feeling skin is an out-an-out prelude to S-E-X, and in female-ese that comment could mean you are thinking about sex with her, yet not about *her*. Don't chance it in these early stages of learning how to reconnect with her.

DO say: "Your skin is so [beautiful, luminous, glowing, amazing; pick one]. I love looking at you." (This way, you are admiring her beauty from afar, in proper worshipful fashion, before sex even occurs to you.)

DON'T say: "I love the way you swing that cute little ass when you walk, honey." It may indeed be a remarkable bum, but ass remarks are lascivious—save them for later when your sex life has heated back up to a rolling boil. Right now, you want to convince her that *she as a whole* is more remarkable than any other woman you know (or any other woman in the world, for that matter).

DO say: "Sweetheart, I love how you move in that dress; you look sixteen again."

> **What, *specifically*, do you find beautiful about her? BE VERBAL: Tell her about it! Just make sure it's not *too* obviously connected to your desire to get her into bed.**

Of course, if you really want to please her (and never veer into the dangerous I-only-really-want-you-for-sex territory), connect to her *face*, if at all possible. For when you think about it, what truly makes each of us unique is what we see looking back at us in the mirror. More than anything else, a woman's face represents to her who she truly is. We women hope and dream that our faces define us as pretty, stunning, impish, sparkly, elegant, etc. That's why as a gender we spend billions of dollars each year on cosmetics and hair products: *We want to make sure we are as beautiful, if not more beautiful, than any woman in the room.* So, if you can manage to find *anything* to like or love about the face we present to the world, please, please tell us; tell us convincingly; and tell us *often*. And when you tell us,

DON'T say: "Hey, what's that glittery blue stuff on your eyes today? It looks neat." For, in female-ese, that remark is about our cosmetic efforts, not about our natural, glorious, beauty (that only takes two hours a day to achieve).

DO say: "Honey, have I ever told you that you have the most incredibly blue eyes? They're so amazing…"

Bingo.

Non-Sexual Physical Actions

Now that you've got an angle on the verbal lovemaking, take the next steps toward the kinds of closeness she needs—extremely important components of active loving.

These actions are more physical, but still must be about closeness, *not about sex*. So: Hold her close by your side as you walk back to the car, as though she's your girl again (which indeed she is) and as though you are the only two people in the world. Then *tell* her she's your girl, too, and take her home for a little wine in front of the fire. Instead of getting comfy in your favorite chairs to watch a movie, grab a blanket for you both and cuddle with her on the sofa, to watch it—just because you want to be close to her, and not because you are expecting anything. And if she's too confused to understand why she's getting all this attention, try it again in a day or two, and then again, until she believes that you are sincere and your attention is not just an aberration!

> **Getting close to your woman may feel awkward at first, but soon you will be back in the habit of being 'with' her, and you won't think about the process, or push it.**

Sooner or later, your sweetheart will come around and trust again that you really, truly love and value her for *her*, and think she is wonderful and beautiful and desirable. Most importantly, soon you will be back in the habit of being with her—*genuinely* being with her—and you will not have to think about the process; you'll enjoy the re-forged connection just as much as she does. Before you know it, the sex will follow as night follows day, for (just as it was when you both started out together) sex is a woman's natural *response* to being actively loved and valued. And when her man wants to connect with her (*love* her) on this kind of level, it's virtually impossible for her *not* to respond.

Persistence is the key. Will you need endless hours each day and each week, to work your way through the kind of loving that your woman needs? Not at all. Certainly, in the beginning you should plan for some of the time you will need. For the remainder, however, grab moments or an hour here or there wherever you can, and don't let yourself miss an opportunity—even a fleeting one. A heartfelt few minutes of genuinely "connecting" with her (even as you cook together, shop for groceries together, or walk the dog) will do more to deepen your relationship and move it back to a physical and sexual level, than the larger, grander gestures you may have been imagining and fearing.

Yet, you'll need to be persistent about this commitment to reconnect with her. Dedicate yourself to it. Don't pass her in the hall without truly noticing her, or stopping to give her a quick hug. Don't look at her face and think to yourself what a pretty woman she still is; *tell* her about it! Don't run out for a quick errand at Sears when you could make it a little lovers' outing and hold hands, talk and laugh at the same time. Think to yourself: *What would you have done years ago, when you were dating her?* To re-establish your connection with your mate, do that again, now!

> **Think: What would you have done when you were dating her? To re-establish your connection with her, do that again, now!**

Once more, you'll need to be careful, at first, that none of your gestures are construed as purely sexual overtures. In the early stages of this new effort, as you re-establish your love connection with your sweetheart, you will need to make sure she cannot accuse you of just trying to get sex from her. To make it easier on yourself, pretend that you are dating her again when sex was not yet in the offing and you were being careful to love her, and yet not scare her off.

That's not dishonest: You *are* genuinely trying to establish love and trust again, to help make sex possible—just as you did when the two of you first started out. It was okay then, and it's perfectly acceptable now to hope that sex is not too far off, as long as your new love connection is genuine.

> **Your mission: To relearn how to achieve connectedness and make your partner feel loved (the way *she* needs it) so that she can make you feel loved (the way *you* need it).**

Your 'Active Love First' Roadmap

Your job is to relearn how to achieve connectedness and make your woman feel loved and valued so that she can respond to you in kind (make you feel loved the way *you* perceive it best). After that, your job is never to forget how to actively "love her first" again!

Briefly, and to make it easy to always be able to connect as described above, here is your roadmap:

First, View Your Actions With a Critical Eye

Don't allow yourself to protect your ego with magical thinking or false assurances. In other words, do not reassure yourself that you *already* give your woman enough focused attention and connecting time each week. Women are much more insecure and needy than you suppose, and men *are* somewhat "relationship lazy" about helping them out. It is simply too easy to tell yourself:

- **She *knows* you love her because you married her** or are her boyfriend.
- **She *seems* pretty contented** with your arrangement.
- **She already *knows* she's good-looking** and desirable.
- **She doesn't need little "gestures of love"** like love notes and gifts anymore, because you have committed to her.

If all of these things were true, you would not be reading this book. And if you are convinced she feels your love via ESP or osmosis, you couldn't be more wrong!

> **Every opportunity you lose to connect with your woman in the way *she* needs it, is time you may forfeit in sexual intimacy with her.**

Instead, go back over the past week or month in your mind and honestly assess your time *alone* with her, connecting, loving, sharing, admiring, and appreciating the partner you have been so lucky to have found.

Of course you can't spend 24 hours a day—or probably even a quarter of each day—actively loving your sweetheart. But there are plenty of opportunities that crop up here and there, each day, each week and each month. Let me put it on a level that cannot be misunderstood: *Every opportunity you lose to connect with your woman is time you will forfeit in sexual intimacy with her.* Conversely, every opportunity to "connect" that you grab and run with, is time that will come back to you in a greater *physical* connection with your sweetheart. It's like building a bridge directly to your bed!

Dedicate the Time
You may need to schedule or plan some of this time, especially at first. And truly connected couples *always* put time on the calendar for their relationship; many even plot that time first and *then* tack on the other commitments—family, friends, work-related. They *first* schedule the time that is most important in their lives: time alone to be together.

In addition to planned time, be determined not to miss the fleeting opportunities for time together. You may be so programmed to walk the dog by yourself that you don't realize those 20 minutes could become very special "together" time. If she balks ("*You're* the dog-walker! It's too cold out!"), turn on the charm the way you would have in those early days, and tell her you just want 20 minutes with your girl and you'll stop at the corner and buy her a latté if she'll be good. Then call her "baby" and give her that grin she fell in love with. If you want to try a little bit of the caveman thing, go ahead and put her hat and coat on for her and drag her from the cave. (Maybe it's been awhile since she's seen that wonderfully commanding side of you?) Remember: No matter how bossy or impossible we women get, *we like our men strong.* Don't let us get away with withdrawing from you.

> **Figure out how much time you may need each week to rebuild love-trust with her. Then double it.**

Bottom line: Figure out how much time you may need each week to start to rebuild love-trust with her. Then double it.

Connect!

Whenever you are alone together, make the time count by focusing your attention on the two of you as an entity. Notice I did not say "focus on her." Of course you need to be paying attention to her by talking, sharing, laughing, remembering—anything that connects you to her and what you would like to share with her, or what you would like her to share with you. Try to choose activities or opportunities that interest you both. But if there is something you know she would love to do, be brave and try a new experience! Be open-minded and let her open her world to you. There is always *something* to appreciate, even in activities that are somewhat alien. (True, chick-flicks may not be your thing. But holding hands during the film is worth the price of admission, and discussing the picture afterward can be fun and even stimulating.) Stepping into *her* world means you are serious about connecting.

Quiet time together is fine, too, as long as you are not distracted (talking on your cell phone, checking your email, watching the game on the TV over the bar, etc.), and as long as you are still emotionally connecting. Remember: If you *look* directly into her eyes, sooner or later you *will* connect with her. Stay focused!

Get Up Close and Personal

With a little luck (and some genuine dedication), you have spent some wonderful time together strolling, reminiscing, laughing and engaging. Suddenly you're sensing feelings of your own that you haven't experienced in quite a while. You want to be close to this woman; to touch her, to feel her, to stroke her cheek and brush her hair off her forehead. Do it! Do it *when* you feel it, *the way* you feel it. The only caveat: Don't be *overtly* sexual (touching breasts, cradling her bottom, placing her hand on your genitals, etc.). Remember: This is about love and tenderness; even about *repressed* lust. But it's not about all-out S-E-X—at least not yet.

[A note about love and repressed lust: I like to recall the evening, years back, when my husband and I were dating and we went out one evening to take in a fascinating lecture. I heard only about 15 minutes of the two-hour talk, even though I had been dying to attend the lecture. All during it, my sweetheart was holding my hand so lovingly, and gently stroking and caressing my palm and each of my fingers, one by one. It was obvious he could barely concentrate on the speaker because he wanted so badly to be connected to me. Not surprisingly, all I can recall about that lecture is my unremitting state of lust for him during those two hours. What happened later that evening falls directly under the heading of "response."]

Where was I? Oh yes... Get close to your sweetheart *at the moment* you feel it, in *the way* that you feel it. This is the time to gaze deeply into her eyes and tell her what you see there; to tell her how you felt when you saw her for the first time. This is the time to tell her what you love most about her, and what you will never forget about her. This is the time to wrap a strong, masculine arm around her and protect her from the world, no matter how headstrong she normally is, or how difficult she's been while the two of you have been "dis-"connected. And this is the time to kiss her the way you really *want* to kiss her. Even if there are people around. Even if the kids are in the next room.

This is the time to take chances and put yourself emotionally "out there." She's been waiting for it for a long time. She may not even remember what it feels like to be with you that way. Take the lead and don't let her back away from that kind of connecting. Guide her back into being in love with you; help her to find that love with you again, just like you did the first time.

> Try kissing her the way you really want to kiss her—even if the kids are in the next room. She's waited a long time for it.

The 'Love First' Seduction Bonus

For those men who don't know it, what I've described in the three paragraphs above not only covers an important how-to about "Actively Loving First," it also forms the critical Act One of seduction, as far as women are concerned. Seduction can quickly move onward from this juncture. But from the woman's point of view, without the "Close and Personal" stage described above (and the breathlessness you should *both* experience), seduction loses its oomph. A relationship zipping along physically may not need as much attention to the critical Act One as you will need to give it in order to rebuild your sex life. But if I were a man, I would *never* omit some form of it, even if that Act One consisted only of a deep kiss and a look of longing—that's how critical to the quality of the sex to come, that first stage of seduction is, to a woman.

Here's a masculine analogy almost any man can understand: It's the difference between being brought to climax by a partner who has given you a few moments of solid "attention" (yes, it means what you think it means), as opposed to a partner who has determinedly teased you along—lovingly, agonizingly, creatively—until you can't stand it a moment longer. To a woman, that Close and Personal stage is the art of seduction at its finest; on a par with the best, unhurried "attention" any man can get before he goes in for the finale. Need more convincing? Then make sure you read Chapter 14, "The Importance of Seducing Your Woman, and How to Do It Right."

Chapter 10
Beauty and Desirability = Sex

The biographies of famous film beauties and sex goddesses (like Marilyn Monroe and Rita Hayworth) have detailed how insecure these women were, especially about their looks—which may be one reason why they needed the adoration of faceless crowds: More than anything, they needed the reassurance that they were, indeed, beautiful.

> Yes, an attractive woman needs to be told often that she *is* attractive, for she doesn't believe it. And an ordinary woman needs you to find her beauty and tell her you see it.

That an attractive woman would need to be told (and told often) that she *is* attractive, is an irony that men have an extremely difficult time grasping. Just as important: That an *ordinary* woman would be hoping her man would find something uniquely beautiful about her to love, is even harder for a man to take seriously.

I believe there are two good reasons for a man's inability to appreciate how central and all-encompassing the "beauty" issue is to a woman's feelings about her desirability.

He Doesn't Get the Beauty Issue: Reason No. 1
In spite of our brains, talents, skills, charms, and ability to compete in the marketplace, women are evolutionarily conditioned to compete for the things that we need in order to survive (a partner, a family, food, shelter, clothing, security) via our ability to attract others through our appearance—our eyes, lips, hair, legs, breasts and derriere, and the way all of those components come

together. Throughout history, the women who could attract men to protect them and fend for them, were often the women who survived best. And though today's woman likes to think that she no longer needs to rely on outward appearances to get what she wants (In the '60s we even tried to convince ourselves that androgynous or unisex was the way to go), the inescapable fact of the matter is that breast enhancements, Brazilian butt-lifts, Botox, over-plumped lips, hair extensions, push-up bras and scanty clothing have never been more in vogue than they are now.

Now, I am not saying that it *should* be this way or even that a woman likes to *admit* that she is programmed to strive for her highest level of beauty in a survival-of-the-fittest world. But the annual sales of the cosmetics, fashion, salon, and fitness industries, not to mention the plastic surgery profession, speak for themselves: By and large, women are at times driven nearly beyond reason in their quest for beauty.

> **The annual sales of cosmetics and plastic surgery speak for themselves: Women are driven to strive for beauty.**

And if you, as a man, feel you cannot relate to our fundamental, inborn need to believe that—on some level—we are beautiful, then let me once again put it to you in a way you may better understand: Women don't *instinctively* understand a man's obsession with the length or girth of his penis, either (after all, to us, a penis has a function and it either functions pretty well or it doesn't). Yet it's a smart, smart woman who accepts that her man's penis is, to him, part of his success and survival in *life*. It secures sex, love, procreation, self-assurance, self-esteem, sometimes even rank or status for him. It gives him release when things get too tough, and gives him comfort when he's feeling unloved or alone. Is it any wonder that he relies on it, reveres it, frets about it—even does whatever it tells him to do, often at an astounding personal cost (loss of wife, girlfriend, job, even political office)? I say it's a smart, smart woman who happily and frequently asserts that her man's penis is more special than any other. After all, his pride and joy exists to ensure her happiness, too.

He Doesn't Get the Beauty Issue: Reason No. 2

The second reason a man finds it difficult to understand how deep the "beauty" issue runs for a woman and her sexuality, is that men are nowhere near as insecure about their looks as women are—a finding that John Gray famously revealed in his book, *Men Are from Mars, Women Are from Venus*[2]. While women usually rank themselves as being less attractive or heavier than they actually are perceived by others, men rank themselves as better looking—often *much* better looking!—than others see them. A man may complain about losing his hair and his muscle tone, and with a 5'7" frame he may weigh in at 190. But ask him how he thinks he ranks next to the average guy, and he'll invariably rank himself around an 8 on a scale of 10.

Not so his lady: She works out like a demon, is a slave to her hair salon, keeps her skin firm and moist, and looks 30 when she's actually eight years beyond. But she sees every tiny wrinkle, stretch mark and split end, not the svelte summer-streaked blonde with the perky breasts and enviable waist. She ranks herself a 6 or a 7, and prays no one will challenge it and peg her closer to a 5.

> You're nowhere near as insecure about your looks as we are. To you, you're always an 8; to us, we're a 6—on a good day.

Is it any wonder you fellas don't quite understand the depth of our need to be beautiful to you? "Hey, you look *fine*, honey," most of you would insist on any given day, because "fine" would be just terrific on your scale, and at least an 8. But in our book, "fine" lingers way down there, near a 4 or 5. And at 4 or 5, we don't deem ourselves desirable to anyone, let alone *you*. In fact, at 4 or 5, it may not be worth getting out of bed in the morning.

What to Do about the Beauty Issue

So what should you do about your woman's deep, fundamental need to feel beautiful in order to feel sexual? Simply put: *Find things to love about how she looks.* Find *specific* things. Concrete things. Things you can *name*. Things that she may, in fact, be proud of. (Does she work hard at those things? Does she spend time and money on them? Has she mentioned them to you?)

> There's something of beauty there—waiting, hoping, *dying* to be noticed. Find it and tell her about it! The more beautiful she feels, the more sensual.

Think hard: Have you ever heard her mention that an old boyfriend thought she had a charming smile or the cutest nose? Does she spend a good deal of time and money at the salon, having her hair kept at just the right shade of luscious russet-red? Does she work hard to keep her skin smooth and glowing? Have you ever noticed that there are flecks of gold in her lovely green eyes? Or are they brown and velvety? Is her neck so swan-like it begs to be kissed? Have you noticed the freckles that skip across the bridge of her nose, just like a little girl's? Are her lips full and pouty and irresistible? Is that little chin adorable? COME ON! There is something of beauty there—waiting, hoping, *dying* to be noticed! Find it, then study it—and study it *hard*. Maybe she'll catch you staring at those gold flecks in her eyes, and you can tell her precisely what you're seeing in her, and just why you love what you see.

And remember: This is about the *uniqueness* of her. This is about what you see as her special, one-of-a-kind attributes. This is about what she is proudest of, as well. It is about *who she is*: her face to the world. (Yes, her gorgeous legs can also be admired at this juncture, but keep boobs and butts out of it, at least at first, or she won't believe that this is about her; she'll think it's about *you* and what *you* want: sex.)

Can you do this? Sure you can! Can you be sincere about what you find to love? Of course you can; you *always* thought those little freckles were totally endearing. You just didn't know she needed to know that you loved them. She does. Tell her now. Tell her often. Find even more to love and appreciate (maybe you'll even decide to put a lovely gold chain around that swan-like neck?). The more you discover to love and the more you let her *know* what you love, the more beautiful and womanly she will feel—and the more sensual.

Chapter 11
Love and Sex, Strength and Power

A terrible thing happens to male/female relationships when men try not to upset their women, and walk on eggshells around them. The balance of the male/female relationship goes kerflooey, and no one ends up happy.

It's often difficult (even for a woman) to understand why we ladies so desperately need our men to retain their strength and power *even as we attempt to erode these things*. My own sense of the dynamic is that women quickly become disappointed, even angry, when they sense that their men can be cowed by them. They swoop in and start to test, test, test, to see if the ground is really as shaky as they sense it is. And whether that test amounts to a cutting remark, a condescending tone, jokes at their man's expense or worse, it all seems diabolically designed to help a woman find out if she has a strong, confident man—or not.

The problem is, we women don't usually realize what we're doing and why we're doing it. A man, however, only knows that while his sweetheart once adored him, now, for some unfathomable reason, she doesn't have much respect for him. Unhappily, once this dynamic is set in motion, his knee-jerk reaction is often to try to appease his lady, stay out of her way, watch his step, weigh his words, or run! All he knows is that life with his love has suddenly gotten more difficult and definitely more bewildering. And it hurts—it truly *hurts*—that he is no longer respected the way he once was. He thought he was her Knight in Shining Armor!

What's so amazing about men is that even if they're feeling disrespected, hurt, and downright unhappy, they *still* will try to please their women and they *still* will try to get physically close to them. (At least, up to a point.)

> **Even if men are feeling disrespected and downright unhappy, they *still* will try to please their women and sleep with them. Not so with the ladies.**

Not so with the ladies. It's a strange irony of life that the person *doing* the disrespecting also feels slighted! She thinks to herself: "I thought I was marrying a strong, masterful man! I've been gypped!" And she doesn't much feel like having sex with a man who seems nervous around her.

There are plenty of Freudian explanations for this sad state of affairs—and it *is* sad because often these couples really do love one another and are genuinely well matched in so many ways. It may have much to do with a woman's need to model her love for a man after the love she may have experienced (or *wish* she had experienced) with a strong, protective father. And conversely, a man's trepidation in the face of his wife's wrath may have much to do with the fact that as a child, all the feminine warmth and nurturing he needed in life came from a being who he could not displease—or else risk losing that essential love.

But honestly, there are no real villains here; there's just behavior—our own and others—that mystifies us and misdirects our relationships, causing no end of problems, not the least of which are problems in the bedroom.

We could say to women—and we *should* say to them—that every time they open their mouths to disparage their men, they should realize that they are testing someone they love, just to find out if he is "worthy" of that love. That kind of "testing" is not only unfair and unkind, it becomes a self-fulfilling prophecy. For sooner or later, a man will tire of the unpleasant treatment and will confirm his wife's or girlfriend's (originally unfounded) suspicions by pulling away from her. Then she can say, "He wasn't worthy of my love after all!"

And we should say to such women that if they would stand by their marriage vows (or their original professions of love) for their mates, and honor and respect their men, then their men—imbued with this confidence from their women—would be stronger for them and more sexually charismatic. Unfortunately, that is another book. *This* book is all about what YOU can do to change the low-sex/no-sex situation you find yourself in and, luckily, when it comes to taking back your power, you can do a LOT.

> **A change in the disrespecting dynamic needs to come from *you* first. Your woman cannot treat you badly unless you let her.**

In fact, any good psychologist will tell you that a change in this male/female dynamic really does need to come from you first. For the truth is that it *is* difficult for a woman to feel sexual about a man she is having trouble respecting even if she is (albeit unwittingly) contributing to the erosion of that respect.

Yet, it is also true that people cannot treat you badly unless you allow them to. Human beings respect those who respect themselves first, last and always. If you will not stand for ill treatment—even from those you love—you will not receive it. If it is attempted, you will deflect it. If those around you have legitimate issues or complaints, you are confident enough to review those issues and hold yourself accountable for the missteps or errors you rightly own; that kind of admission does nothing to erode your strength, it only enhances it.

People who are that secure in their relationships with others are people with well-formed, healthy psyches. If you find yourself too often apologizing for your existence, fending off sharp-tongued attacks, or avoiding situations that may turn sour—*even with, or especially with, your own mate*—then it is time to take back your power and do something about the state you find yourself in.

> **The woman who loves you is waiting for you to stand up for yourself and refuse to be ill-treated. Even by her. *Especially* by her.**

First and foremost, the woman who loves you is waiting for you to stand up for yourself and refuse to be ill-treated. Even by her. *Especially* by her.

Yet what if you are having trouble distinguishing which circumstances are actually unfair to you, and which situations you need to be accountable for? Learn to take a "time out" to remove yourself from a situation, in order to assess it. You have a right to take that time; everyone does. As soon as possible, though, return and deliver your own verdict on the situation. Either way, whether you can calmly respond on the spot, or take some small amount of time and *then* return to respond, your interaction could go something like this:

> **She says:** "I can't believe you forgot to pick up the dry cleaning again! Can't you remember *anything*?"
>
> **You say:** "I did forget to pick it up, and I apologize. Now I would like *you* to apologize for speaking to me like I'm a child instead of your husband. And I'll be happy to pick up the cleaning later today when I go out. And I promise not to treat *you* badly when *you* forget something."
>
> Tone of voice is important: Be calm, be kind, but be *assured*. You wouldn't let a coworker speak to you as nastily as your own partner did, would you?

Here's another potential scenario:

> **She says:** (To a friend, in your presence.) "Oh John can be such a dope. I have to tell him over and over again that bath towels do *not* get folded back onto the rods when they're wet!"

You either:
a) Politely remove yourself from the situation and wait until later when you are alone with your wife/girlfriend, to let her know that her behavior was entirely unacceptable.
b) Request your mate's presence in the other room ("Excuse me. Mary, may I see you in the other room for a moment?") Then quietly let your lady know that her behavior is unacceptable.

If you can manage option A, it is probably preferable so that you do not embarrass the friend. But if your wife or girlfriend has been continually misbehaving where you're concerned, then the friend is probably already embarrassed (mostly for your lady's bad behavior and your own wimpiness in not stopping it). So, go ahead and put an end to the situation quickly and cleanly, and if you handle it firmly and fairly, you'll gain a lot of respect instantly.

When alone with your mate, say firmly but calmly:
"Please don't talk that way about me, to anyone, ever again. It's unacceptable behavior and I would *never* treat you that way, no matter how many silly things you did. You're not perfect and neither am I; no one is. But I do have a solution where the towels are concerned: If you hang your own towels the way you like and stop worrying about mine, I'll be more than happy to handle something that *you* don't like to do, like [take out the garbage, get the car oil changed, etc.]."

Always deal with the issues at hand, and never name-call or make the discussion personal. ("I've had it with you! Everyone thinks you're such a bitch!") The point is: *You are a man who is perfectly happy with himself,* one who does his best to be kind and to share tasks. You were created as a man, not a woman, and you cannot effortlessly see things as she does, nor do you expect your partner to expertly manage all of the things for which you, a man, might have a greater affinity. You do not bully her (I hope!) and you will not permit her to bully you *on any level*.

> **If you think you are being 'accommodating' by putting up with her misbehavior, you are only fooling yourself and, ironically, you are also alienating her affections.**

A Final Word of Warning

Be cautioned: If you think you are just being "accommodating" to your woman by putting up with her misbehavior ("Oh, Jenna can be a little difficult at times, but it doesn't really bother me..."), you are fooling only yourself, for everyone else is aware that she is a bully and that you have made the choice to become her doormat. What's more, whether you can see it or not, by refusing to take back your power, you are actually *alienating* her affections. And, as a result, you are ruining your life and hers in the bedroom.

Your lady doesn't want accommodation of her bad behavior. She doesn't want to end up despising herself *and* you. She wants a man. She wants you to take back your power and strength, fairly and benevolently.

Do not disappoint her!

Chapter 12
The Nearness (The Maleness!) of You

Way back in 1938, composer Hoagy Carmichael and lyricist Ned Washington wrote the unforgettable tune, "The Nearness of You,"[3] later to be performed by Mel Tormé, Etta James, Sarah Vaughan, Frank Sinatra, Ella Fitzgerald, Norah Jones and Diana Krall, among other jazz greats.

There's a reason the tune has endured—no, *thrived*—through each and every decade: It flawlessly captures the essence of what has eternally fueled the best kind of sexual intimacy between men and women. Look at the lyrics:

> Why do I just wither and forget all resistance
> When you and your magic pass by
> My heart's in a dither, dear
> When you are at a distance
> But when you are near, oh my

> It's not the pale moon that excites me
> That thrills and delights me, oh no
> It's just the nearness of you

> It's not your sweet conversation
> That brings this sensation, oh no
> It's just the nearness of you

> When you're in my arms and I feel you so close to me
> All my wildest dreams come true

> I need no soft lights to enchant me
> If you'll only grant me the right
> To hold you ever so tight
> And to feel in the night the nearness of you

It's all about physical proximity, isn't it? On the surface of things, that may seem like a no-brainer to you, for you'll insist you just *love* to get close to your honey—especially in the bedroom but, alas, nowadays she just won't cooperate!

> **Women often say they feel disconnected and lonely for their man's physical 'nearness.' If you only offer that in the bedroom, it's way too late to connect to her.**

Well, here's my newsflash for you: Your lady will probably say that she feels disconnected; detached from you; maybe even lonely for your physical "nearness." And as we've said before, if you're waiting until you get *into* the bedroom to let your woman feel the "nearness" of you, you're waiting way, way too long to connect to her, and that may be one big reason why you're not getting her into that bed in the first place. Look again at these lyrics:

My heart's in a dither, dear
When you are at a distance
But when you are near, oh my

It's not the pale moon that excites me
That thrills and delights me, oh no
It's just the nearness of you

She's saying that her heart doesn't know what to do "When you are at a distance." "*But when you are near, oh my ... It's just the nearness of you*" that excites her!

In other words: Long before sex is on the horizon for her, it is feeling your physical nearness, your *maleness* (e.g., your scent, the larger size of you compared to her own frame; the tautness of your body as opposed to the softness of her own; your strong arms) right next to her femaleness, that gets her libido in gear! That means: While it's perfectly appropriate to be that close in the bedroom, can you imagine how sexy and flame-fanning it would be for her to feel your body (even fully clothed—*especially* fully clothed) close to hers, in a situation *where sexual overtures have not yet been made*?

> It's your nearness, your scent, the tautness of your body right next to hers that gets her in gear. She needs to feel how different her feminine body is from your masculine one.

Vive La Difference

Now, you notice that my reference to "maleness" did not include the obvious. That's because first—before anything physical, um, changes for you—a woman needs simply to feel how different and how *masculine* your body feels to her, to help her start to be aware of how feminine her own body is feeling to *her*. We've spoken many times about female sexual response, and about how important a woman's response mechanisms are to her sexual ignition processes. Well, just as a man starts to feel truly sexual when he is aroused, *a woman needs that chance to feel her own arousal, too!* And if you are confronting her with *your* arousal process, she's got too little time to get tuned in to her own, slow-burning arousal process and nurture it. To put it plainly: She has no time to fan her own flame!

> Learn how to bridge your daily physical distance from her and get 'near' to her in *non*-sexual situations. It makes her think about you, miss you, long for you, *want* you.

So, instead of pouncing on your lady the moment you're in the mood for sex (or indicating that you'd like sex to be forthcoming), learn how to bridge your daily physical distance from her and get "near" to her in *non*-sexual situations, even situations that cannot immediately become intimate because of logistics (you are at a restaurant, in a park, with friends, etc.).

The "nearness" of your maleness, *with no overt sexual expectation*, gives your mate the chance to breathe in every male nuance of you, and have the luxury of enjoying your physicality for its own sake. It *connects* her to you. It makes her think about you, miss you, long for you and *want* you. (It's as heady as a drug!) And it gives her the *time* she needs for all of that (even if it turns out she only needs seconds). Most important of all, it gives her time to desire you and then fan that desire, without you knocking her over with yours.

> **Physical 'nearness'—without the immediate opportunity for sex—gives her the time to desire you and fan that desire, without you knocking her over with yours.**

Before It Got Easy, It Was Agony

Does "nearness" sound like an alien concept to you? It's not; it's the way things were for centuries, before sexual behaviors changed dramatically in the 1960s. Prior to the sexual revolution of the '60s, people could be near each other and, yet, they could not have each other. In earlier decades and centuries, there was dating (with chaperones, early on), bundling (lying together but not touching) and courting (some kissing and hugging allowed).

Best of all, there was dancing (that wonderful, glorious "vertical expression of a horizontal desire") and to romantic music, to boot. Is it any wonder that during two World Wars couples met, danced, and then ran off to be married in only days? Their physical "nearness" on the dance floor with none of that (later to come) 1960s lets-jump-into-the-sack convenience, made it *unbearable* not to be able to make love. And the torture of nearness was not just agony for men; *women* couldn't stand physical closeness without consummation, either! In those days, the only way to control those flames of desire was to get married—fast!

> **Dancing was the original mode of 'nearness' without sex. Is it any wonder couples met, danced, then ran off to be married in only days? The 'nearness' was unbearable.**

Yet, somewhere along the way, with the help of the sexual revolution, both men and women lost that wonderful agony of nearness with its delayed consummation. And while men can still get their fires going at the drop of a hat any day or night of the week, it's we women who have lost so much. We have lost our shot at the nearness that helps us to percolate *prior* to sexual overture. And (especially with our hectic, busy lifestyles where couples can go for days and weeks with barely a physical touch between them) modern romance suffers greatly as women get less and less nearness time to want and desire their men. Oh dear, whatever is a girl to do?

As it often happens, nothing. She waits for her chances for the non-sexually motivated nearness that will help her move into her sexual response, but she doesn't always get it. What she does get, however, are directly sexual overtures with little or no time for her own feminine brand of warming up and sexual self-awareness. It's no one's fault but, once again, your sweetheart is expected to be sexual in the way a *man* is, and it's just not working for her. Worse, she's feeling inadequate as she just can't heat up like she did some time back, and she wonders, often miserably, why the sexual encounter is moving right along without her full participation. You can change all that, and so very easily, too.

Making 'Nearness' Happen for Her
Just let her feel your physical being, more often. Get up close to her. Put your arm (or arms) around her and let her feel your phys-

ical presence and how manly you are, so that she can get in touch with her own femininity, in comparison. Give her a non-sexual hug and let her feel how broad your chest is, and how muscular against her softness. Take her little hand in yours and let her feel the strength, and yet the manly gentleness, in your touch. Pull her close to you as you walk down the street, and let her feel your protectiveness as you guard her and keep her from harm. All of these things make your sweetheart feel so feminine alongside your masculinity. The difference she then senses *in herself* makes her hormones begin to simmer and then surge (which takes a little more time than it does for you!).

> **Today, what she often gets is sexual overture with little time for her own brand of warming up. It makes her feel she's just not as sexual as she was some time ago.**

In addition, if you learn to keep yourself physically "connected" to your woman when no immediate sexual encounter is in the offing, it will build sexual trust between you. She will believe that you love her for *her*, and not just for sex. And so (in that crazy, female, upside-down world she lives in, where she doesn't necessarily accept that sex IS how you show you love her) she will be so much more open to sex when you do initiate it. She will even find it so hard to get you out of her mind after savoring the Nearness of You, that she will initiate encounters herself! And wouldn't *that* be the icing on the cake...

> **She needs to believe that you love her for *her*, not sex, so that (in that crazy upside-down world she lives in) she will be so much more open to sex when you do initiate it.**

So slip a loose rubber band around your wrist to train yourself to get physically close to your lady for no other reason than to be close to her (and make her want you): Every time you notice the band on your wrist, put your arm around her or reach out and stroke her little face with your big, manly hand. And if you're at the office and she's at home and you can't reach out and physically hold her, go ahead and send her a text or email hug. It's the next best thing to the Nearness of You.

Chapter 13
The Happiness of Pursuit

Ever heard the term "hot pursuit"? Well they don't call it "hot" for nuthin', honey.

Yes, I know: Those two words are commonly used together to refer to the exciting police chases you see on TV. But utter that term near a woman—almost any woman—and her little brain cells will start conjuring up the kind of man-wants-woman chase that will get her hormones pumping in a flash. That must be the way it is, for romance novel plots are *constructed* around hot pursuit, and romance novel publishers make a LOT of money. The truth is, when it comes to eliciting a sexual response from a woman (and for her, sex is *all* about response), there's nothing like pursuit.

> **The truth is, when it comes to eliciting a sexual response from a woman, there's just nothing like pursuit.**

Yet, what kind of pursuit are we talking about? For your sweetheart, pursuit can mean the dogged quest with which you first went after her (remember how you never gave up when she ignored your first pick-up line, your first suggestions of a drink or dinner, your first advances?). Or (assuming you have used Chapters 1 through 12 to fully reconnect to her) it can mean a surprisingly physical and determined Sunday afternoon chase around the sofa, kitchen table, and bed while the kids are downtown at a movie matinee. It can even mean a fixed gaze across a room during a party, followed by an impulsive dash to a veranda, away from prying eyes. Your "hot" pursuit can be your sheer inability to resist the urge to reach over to her, remove the clip from her hair, and run your hand through her tresses as they tumble down. But no matter how you decide to pursue her, how much she feigns disinterest, or how loudly she shrieks in delighted protest, remember this: Once the two of you have reconnected, hot pursuit becomes the polar *opposite* of the dreaded sexual "expectation"—at least as far as she is concerned.

> **Hot pursuit is the polar opposite of the dreaded sexual 'expectation.'**

Unlike your Saturday night pronouncement, "Hey, let's go in the bedroom" or your late-night entreaty, "Honey, are you asleep?" hot pursuit doesn't *expect* anything, *ask* for anything, or—worst of all—*beg* for anything. Hot pursuit immediately transmits that you are man, she is woman, and eons of biologically unstoppable hooking-up must prevail!

Most of all, it indisputably conveys that you find her womanly, attractive, desirable, adorable, *irresistible*—all of the things she hopes and dreams of being to you. And it tells her that she is, in fact, *so* feminine that she brings out the caveman in you and you simply cannot help yourself: You must have her!

Then too, chasing your lady until you catch her says so many important things about *you* that may have gotten lost somewhere along the way. Your pursuit of her says that you are: *Determined.* You are *confident* you will prevail. You are *assured* of your own *power* to thrill and then possess her. You are entirely comfortable with your *masculinity,* and *proud* of it. Pursuing her says: *You will not be kept from the woman you love and desire.*

Were you paying attention to those words in italics? Isn't that the man you've always wanted to be? Well, that's the man *she* wants you to be, too, no matter how deeply ingrained her resistant ways have become. You've taken the time and effort to reestablish your active love connection with her, now just give her time to get back in touch with the joy of being pursued again, and don't take no for an answer—she'll come around before you know it.

> **Your pursuit means you want her and need her and are willing to *work* to get her—which is what all women really, truly, deeply want from their men, in order to respond sexually.**

Pursuit 'Transmissions'
Yes, you should by all means be determined to catch your woman, hold her in your arms, kiss her and (when you can tell she's warming to your game) make passionate love to her. But should your hot pursuit of her be deadly serious? Hell no; you don't want to scare the dickens out of her! This kind of pursuit is a love game: it's romantic; it's fun; it's the best kind of prelude to very good sex—full of laughter, anticipation, and excitement. It means you want her and need her and are willing to *work* to get her—which is what you convinced her of, once upon a time, when you first went after her. Most importantly, *it's what all women deeply desire from their men, in order to respond to them sexually*. Over and over again. For as long as you are willing to show her that you want her enough to run after her until she lets you catch her.

> **The sexual 'transmissions' she picks up during pursuit will feel like a pulsating barrage she can't help but respond to.**

In fact, all the sexual "transmissions" your lady will pick up during your pursuit of her (your determination, confidence, power, masculinity, refusal to be kept from the irresistible object of your desire) will feel to her like a pulsating barrage that she cannot help but respond to physically.

And if you think about it quite honestly (keeping in mind that a woman *must* have something to respond to, in order to function sexually), you may even end up asking yourself how she has been able to call up her sexuality for you in recent times (if she has), when you have pretty much been lying on the sofa, watching her go by, wishing that she would sleep with you one of these days—and not giving her the man/woman cue of pursuit that you now know she desperately craves.

> **It took two of you to dig your sexual rut: Yes, you forgot how to drag her back to the cave, but she has been reminding you in all sorts of ways that you are disappointing her.**

Yet, don't blame yourself for the rut that you may have fallen into—it took two of you to keep digging that trench. *You* may have forgotten how to be a real caveman and drag her back to the cave, but *she* (in her misery at being so undesirable) has made sure to remind you in all sorts of ways that you were disappointing her. She may even have tried to erode your masculinity at every turn, since you were not flexing that masculinity for her, anyway. (Strange female reasoning, I know.) So…

Plan Your Pursuit!
Think again about pursuing her. Think about how you might do it, lying in wait just like a tiger, waiting for your opportunities. Consider starting small: The kids are in bed; you and she haven't started your own dinner yet; she heads into the bedroom to change her shoes and you follow her silently and lock the bedroom door behind you, just loud enough for her to hear. She turns around. You pull her gently toward you (while she protests about dinner, the kids, etc., etc.), but you are not to be deterred from your mission. You bury your face in her hair and whisper, "Come here, you; I've been dying to do this all day, and this time I'm not going to let you run away from me. I just want to hold you in my arms and feel you close to me. You look so beautiful tonight…"

How does this differ from those earlier scenarios where you grabbed a "cheek" as she was cooking dinner or poked at "the girls"? It differs in this way: Here, you have been actively loving and valuing her and have reestablished your connection to her, first. What's more, you are not making this about *your* general need for sex. Here, in her eyes, you are making this all about your love and desire for *her*. It's all about *her*, and about how much you need *her*. Here, you are expressing your primal need to connect with her touch, her scent, her warmth, her beauty. The dash to the cave comes afterward, as her insecurity (that you just want *any* warm body for sex) is thoroughly allayed, and she's genuinely convinced that her man adores *her* and is, at long last, back.

The irony: Back in that first scenario in the kitchen, you *did* want her to know that you wanted only her. The difference is that, then, you approached her with male-ese, instead of female-ese; you approached her with no connection (that she could understand) first. Here, she actually comprehends and feels what you were trying to let her know earlier: That you love her, you think she's wonderful and, *thus*, you want to connect with her, badly.

Finally, you've rediscovered how to connect with your sweetheart in a way that means everything wonderful to her. And in a way that will make her completely open to you, and ready for—hurrah!—her sexual response.

Now, the only question is: Will her sexual response be "nice," or mind-blowing? The answer is entirely up to you (with a little help from me).

Chapter 14
The Importance of Seducing Your Woman, and How to Do It Right

You've reconnected. You've pursued. You've prevailed. You have her respect again—and her awe. She suspects that she is putty in your hands, and you've been happy to reinforce that belief with your show of strength and desire, and your willingness to work for your woman in order to possess her, body and soul.

You could stop your back-to-bed training right here, and have a perfectly fine love life. Or, you could become a *master* and have her eating out of your, ah, hand...

> **Why have sex that is perfectly fine, when you (yes, I mean YOU) could easily learn to seduce your woman into the kind of sex life you have only dreamed about?**

In other words, you (yes, I mean YOU) could learn to *seduce* your woman into the kind of sex life you have only dreamed about. And you won't even have to buy brown-paper-wrapped books to make it happen for, no matter what some guy at a bar in 1998 told you, seducing a woman you have long been carnally involved with (and very possibly, women in general) is *not* about sexual techniques. Yes, you heard me right.

The Difference Between Sex and Seduction
Most men mistakenly believe that seducing their woman relies solely on a superior knowledge of sexual technique, because—in the American culture, anyway—seduction and the sex act are al-

ways lumped together. In my own experience, it's been a challenge indeed to get a man to understand that seduction *can* involve some initial sexual interplay but, for women, the true art of seduction may not involve direct sexual contact at all. As far as we women are concerned, only *sex* is sex; seduction isn't sex too; it is what *leads to* sex—that is, if you're at all good at seduction.

> As far as women are concerned, only sex is sex. Seduction isn't sex; it's what *leads* to sex—if you're at all good at seduction.

As we've seen earlier, the original concept of seduction is that of *leading astray* or *enticing* into sexual intercourse. Nowhere is seduction defined as intercourse (or a sex act) itself. Throughout history, the men who were the greatest lotharios or "corrupters" of women were those who were somehow able to get women to *want* to give themselves to them, even if it meant ruination. These men weren't necessarily handsome, powerful or wealthy, but they certainly understood women and how to set them on fire. The pages of history are littered with women who have thrown themselves at their seducers before these men even lifted a skirt for a peek. And in modern times, in mass rock-concert seductions, women have tossed their panties at rock stars they've never even *met*! How do real-life lady killers do it?

Indirectly. They do it through the acquired art of Attention, Suggestion, Promise, Withholding and the staving-off of sexual delivery while the Attention, Suggestion, Promise, Withholding cycle is repeated and *both* parties' imaginations expand the promise by fantastic proportions.

Does this sound familiar to you? If your reading of the lines above got you thinking about the sex act itself, there's a very good reason for that: It's because the art of seduction is very much like the art of very, very good sex: Great sex employs *Attention* to erogenous zones, the *Suggestion* of more attention to come, the *Promise* and delivery of even more physical attention, the *Withholding* of the ultimate attention (bordering on the excruciating), and the ongoing feeding of the imagination to help build excitement to indescribable heights.

The big difference between the sexual encounter itself and well-played seduction, is that true seduction gains its real power from sexual *abstinence*, leaving sex as the next stage altogether. Furthermore, the eventual sexual encounter is made even more potent by the "virtual" (*not* directly sexual) state of the seduction.

The Joy of Seduction

Think about it: Maybe that's why phone sex is such a powerful aphrodisiac for many men and women alike. There's the fact that the caller is paying Attention *only* to the recipient of the call; then there's all that lurid Suggesting going on about the Promise of what will happen later. And of course there's a whole lot of Withholding in the mix, during all that talk, talk, talk and by virtue of the fact that the two parties are not even physically in each others' presence!

Many actively sexual couples employ sexy phone calling during the day from locations where no consummation of any kind could possibly take place (an office where others can view them through a glass door, for instance; or standing on a street corner quietly whispering into a cell phone as others pass by), *specifically* to heighten anticipation and let it build throughout the day—guaranteeing a memorable crescendo shortly after being reunited in the evening.

For a man as well as for a woman, seduction is a miraculous thing, and men absolutely adore being seduced by their women. The only difference is: While a strip tease or a sexy phone call is unquestionably appreciated by a man, it's not necessarily vital to his performance. The fact of the matter is, a man can enjoy fabulous sex without any formal seduction at all—a peek at a bra strap, a flash of thigh, or a fleeting thought can often be all the seduction he needs to get going.

> **For a woman, some level of seduction makes all the difference—and the more artful the seduction, the more memorable the ensuing sexual encounter will be.**

Yet for a woman (whose sexual response has been said to be more like that of a slow-heating oven, as opposed to a man's ultra-fast microwave), some level of seduction makes all the difference—and the more artful the seduction, the more memorable the ensuing sex will be.

Despite what you may believe, women (even *your* reticent lady) love to lose themselves in sex and make love with wild abandon. And isn't that your dream come true? It turns out that how well you seduce (even if that seduction comprises all of four minutes, but is artfully done) may mean the difference between a cozy ten minutes in bed or an hour or two of passionate lovemaking.

The most important thing to remember: While men enjoy direct stimulation in sex and directness in a woman's manner of seducing them (think striptease), many women (especially those who have been out of the sex loop for a while) favor *in*direct stimulation in both realms. On a physical level (if you're well-versed or well-read in sexual technique), you know what I mean when it comes to clitoral stimulation, for instance: Many women cannot tolerate direct stimulation at all. And it's a similar situation when it comes to female seduction. Grabbing at her breast out of nowhere and muttering "How about it?" just doesn't cut it for most women; in truth, it can be off-putting.

Of course, if you and your lady have a super-heated sex life and she's always fired up, easily fired up, or loves to get *you* fired up (in which case you're not reading this book), then by all means make those phone-sex calls or sidle up to her and whisper unspeakable acts of sexual depravity in her ear; she may even beat you to the bedroom. But if there is any sexual distance between you, you'll need to more shrewdly ignite the embers of her fire, and then keep building that fire like the good Boy Scout you are, so that it doesn't wane or burn too rapidly to enjoy.

For you, my friend, indirect is definitely the way to go. Practice the following steps of Attention, Suggestion, Promise, and Withholding, and you'll know how to ignite and stoke her fires forever.

> If you're only handing out attention when sex crosses your mind, she'll be convinced you don't care about her the other 23 hours a day, and want her just for sex.

Step One (Part 1): General Attention
Once again, the thing to remember about attention is this: If you only hand it out as a preface to sex, eventually your lady will catch on (sorry, but she's got antennae). She'll catch on *and* she'll end up resenting you. For the life of them, men can't understand why women would be angry about getting romantic attention when their men are thinking about them sexually. But as in most things with women, it's not about what you ARE doing, it's about what you're NOT doing. And if you're only paying attention to your woman or showing her affection when sex crosses your mind, she'll quickly become convinced that you don't care about her during the other 23 hours of each day; you want her just for sex.

Rather than trying to persuade her that this way of thinking and feeling is crazy (or rather than avoiding the issue altogether because you've decided her reaction has no merit), why not learn how to venture out of that Never-Never Land (where the *Lost Boys* are, remember?) and give her a really good man-hug as she walks by you in the kitchen, den, wherever? Or, maybe set aside time during your busy day to go for a walk, hold hands, and just talk about nothing. Or mute the TV volume during a long commercial break, pull her onto your lap and tell her that you missed her and want to know how her day was. Bottom line: If you have four to five hours after work and before bedtime each day, be generous with a small portion of it!

> **If your lady rarely glanced at you, touched you, or paid attention to you during the week, would you be happy to respond to her sudden request for some luxury item?**

Think about it this way: If your lady rarely glanced at you, touched you, or paid attention to you during the week, would you be happy to respond to her sudden request for some luxury item she was hankering for? Would you be so eager to make *her* happy after a week of such limited attention from her?

Again, I'm not saying that her sexual favors should be a "gift" to you—they shouldn't! But the fact of the matter is that if you're not being generous with *your* time and attention, she may not feel generous about the time and attention she shares with *you*. That's just the way women (and human beings, in general) are.

So, practice giving her non-sex-related attention regularly ("active loving": attention and affection *especially* when sex is not in the offing) and she will be so much more receptive to your pre-sex attention, when you trot it out.

Then, learn how to master *pre*-sex attention.

Step One (Part 2): Mastering *Pre*-sex Attention

Pre-sex attention differs from non-sex-related attention in that it starts out as non-sex-related attention, but gradually or quickly (depending on your skill at sensing your woman's reactions) turns heady and more intense. In essence, it deepens and becomes more romantic and then ripe with suggestion. (Even its *description* sounds sexy, doesn't it?)

Take the following scenario. Yup, we're in the kitchen once again but, this time, instead of bounding up behind her and grabbing at her with overt "I-wanna-have-sex-with-you" moves (our first kitchen setting), things progress in a way that works so much more effectively for your lady's slow-to-heat-up, do-you-really-love-me libido. Here's how it goes:

You are home from work, making some drinks for the two of you, while your wife is getting dinner ready in the kitchen. (The kids are in summer camp, at the neighbors, or haven't been born yet.) As she moves by you, you notice she's wearing a particularly nice outfit. You put the drinks down on the counter and gaze at her. "Hey," you say. She looks up, questioningly. "You look amazing today," you tell her.

She blushes. "I do?"

You nod. "You sure do, honey. I haven't seen that top before, have I?"

> **She's not only got your *full* attention now, she's also got your admiration: You think she's beautiful! You're her hero again.**

Notice that you're not speaking in generalities, here. (Why go with the generic "You look nice" when you can find something to be *specific* about, and thus be believable.)

You go on: "You know, you look really beautiful in red. I remember you wore red the first time we met. I couldn't take my eyes off you." (She's not only got your *full* attention now, she's also got your admiration: You think she's beautiful! You're her hero again.)

"Oh, sweetie—" she utters, blushing some more, and trying to go on about her work.

"Come here," you gently insist, lowering your voice so that she knows you mean business.

"I'm making *dinner!*" she protests, this time unconvincingly. (Her part of the mating dance: resistance.) Now it's time for you to move on to...

Step Two: Suggestion
"Dinner can wait," you announce in a way that tells her she's so captivating, you can't think about things like food at the moment. "Why don't you turn off that stove," you finally command. (Ooh—a masterful command; hooray for you!) You sidle up to her, flip off the burner knob and put your arms around her. Then you lift her hair from her neck, unhurriedly feel her silky skin with your fingertips, and kiss her gently and lingeringly along her nape.

She pretends to struggle with the saucepan. "But what about our spaghetti?" she giggles nervously.

> **Your well-chosen words tell her that your sexual feelings are specifically about *her*, and not just about needing sex.**

"You shouldn't have worn this outfit," you barely whisper (being *specific* again). "You look just like you did the first day we met." (In other words—and importantly—your sexual feelings are about *her*, and *specifically* about her, and not just about needing sex.) With one hand you take the saucepan from her grasp and park it on the corner of the range. You slowly turn her around, put your arms around her again, and hold her tightly (after all, you're *serious!*). You kiss her deeply but softly on the lips, and *wait to feel her response*. (Important: Don't take off on this ride without her! Don't be oblivious to her heat and her signals.)

Then her response comes: She puts her arms around your neck and kisses you back.

> You decide to take her for a roller-coaster ride she'll not soon forget; you show her you want to get lost in seduction with her.

At this point, you *could* pick her up and dash to the bedroom (and if your sex life were already hot as blazes, why not?), OR you could take her for a little roller-coaster ride she'll not soon forget, and show her that you care enough to get lost in seduction with her. You decide to do just that and torture both of you deliciously. You move on to—

Step Three: Promise
Instead of what she might expect (grabbing her and jumping her bones), you masterfully and determinedly nudge her up against the kitchen wall. You lean against her and kiss her some more. But this time (I know: It's *so* not like you!) you get really into those kisses—first kissing her softly and lusciously and really tasting her lips, then kissing her more deeply and lovingly, then more passionately, then doing it all over again, tracing her lips carefully and lingeringly. (So *this* is what "making out" is all about! You haven't done this since high school. Maybe you've *never* done it. Don't delay; now's the time!)

> So *this* is what 'making out' is all about! You haven't done this since high school. Maybe you've *never* done it. Now's the time!

Your body is right up against hers; she can feel your heat, you can feel hers, and you can both feel anything else that's changing shape between you. She is of course expecting you to move head-first into man-handling—after all, she *is* your woman and your hands once knew her territory well. She is certain that even though you are professing admiration for *her*, you pretty much want sex as soon as you can obtain it.

But that's where she's wrong. You don't man-handle her at all. You truly are lost in her kisses and the sound of her breaths; in the sound of her heart beating against your chest; the feel of her cheek against your own. The side of your hand may just lightly—*by pure accident, mind you*—brush against the curved outer edge of her breast or the very tip of it, as it moves downward to the outside of her thigh (*not* the inside of her thigh, which is directly sexual). There, your hand gently pushes up her skirt, merely to feel the skin beneath it (just like a Victorian suitor, hoping for a meager glimpse of flesh). Your hand strokes the silkiness of her thigh, or it even allows her skirt to fall again so that you can reach behind her and trace the curve of her lovely bottom with the cup of your palm.

She's breathing heavily, now. You are making both of you crazy.

If all of this sounds like the kind of banned book you paid good money for back in 19__ when you were 13 years old, then you now understand why women love romance novels: This stuff is hot! And it's hot because it's A-G-O-N-Y.

Luckily for you, right about now she is whispering in your ear, "Honey, honey, let's go in the bedroom..." Or maybe she is even trying to undo your belt buckle. (Meanwhile, you are hearing strains of the Hallelujah Chorus in the distance.) You can feel her heat blasting right through the front of your shirt. So of course you move on to—

Step Four: Withholding
Now, no one is suggesting you call a screeching halt to the activities here; that would be insanity! In truth, withholding is a very delicate operation and has to approximate the smooth-as-silk downshifting of a finely tuned sports car heading into a bend at 80 mph.

So, at this point you're both breathing heavily and moving into that bend at high speed. Again she utters, "honey, honey—" but you move your hand away from where it was fondling her sweet little derriere, take hold of her little chin instead (her fault for interrupting you!) and whisper, "ssshhh, ssshhh, kiss me. You're making me crazy—"

And that may be all the withholding necessary, before she all but carries *you* into the bedroom.

Withholding is meant to push you both just the teeniest bit past the point where you already thought you couldn't take any more, and it takes practice to get it just right. But the best thing about withholding is: If you are doing it right, you're actually seducing your woman to the point where she may take things into her own hands. (Pun intended.) Withholding is also designed to help heat up a partner who warms up slowly or hasn't heated up in quite some time. So you may, in fact, want to go from withholding back into Attention, Suggestion, and Promise—and then, of course to delivery.

> **The key to much of seduction is to progress *together*—taking *both* of your temperatures as you move forward. When there is plenty of activity from her side, too, move ahead!**

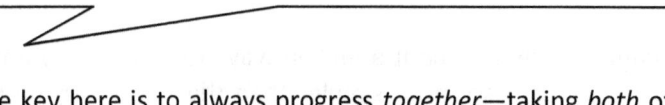

The key here is to always progress *together*—taking *both* of your temperatures as you move forward. You take her temperature (and yours, too, for that matter), by getting lost in the breathing, whispering, touching, sighing, and heat emanating from both of you. (An important note here: If all of the activity is coming from you alone, you need more seduction practice or some regrouping and re-studying of this book as a whole.) If there is plenty of activity coming from her side, as well, then you are a lucky boy and you should not torture the two of you any longer than is absolutely necessary. Full steam ahead! Move on to delivery! (And don't neglect to practice *more* seduction techniques later, to thrill her even more, next time around.)

Broaden Your Seduction Horizons

You've now read through the above scenario two or three times, and you're wondering if you can scrawl crib notes on the inside of your palm, because you're certain you're not going to get all the details right. Hey, you don't have to do *any* of the above. Or, you can try out my little imaginary scene, verbatim, just to see if it really works. Then lose it.

> There are many ways to seduce a woman, and most of them are pretty darn simple. Just don't keep doing it *the same way*—unless you want it to be *non*-seductive.

I say "lose it," because seduction is a funny thing: No matter how beautifully you perform it, if you've carried it out precisely the same way once before (or, at least, within her recent memory), it suddenly becomes *non*-seductive, no matter how impeccable your skill. So, resist the temptation to reuse your ol' favorite "tried-and-true" seduction approach! (Sorry, fellas, this is one time you can't keep going back to the store for red roses or your standby chocolates, if you get my somewhat harsh analogy.)

Fortunately, there are about a million ways to seduce a woman, and many of them are a lot simpler than the kitchen scene detailed above. In fact, with the help of Matt and Emma below, I can reduce an entire seduction scenario to a look, a touch, four words, a kiss, and a sigh:

Matt looks up from the paper and truly *sees* his love, Emma, sitting across the table from him. She glances back at him; he is gazing at her so intently. He reaches for her hand and holds it as though he never has before. "You're so beautiful tonight," he tells her, taking in her eyes, her mouth, her lovely hair—and meaning it. They gaze at each other for a number of moments. Then he kisses the inside of her hand and gently returns it to her. He winks and reluctantly goes back to the paper. "Oh, Matt..." Emma sighs.

If you think about it, you'll realize there are endless ways to seduce a woman—and *endless seduction opportunities that present themselves for the taking*. If there weren't, the film industry would have gone belly-up decades ago, because boy meets girl, boy chases girl, girl resists boy, boy catches girl is seduction in itself, and is what all women wish their men would not have forgotten, the moment they said "I do," "I love you" or anything similar.

If you're a student of film history, somewhere along the way you may have rented the award-winning 1963 film, *Tom Jones*[4], and watched the famously lascivious dinner scene the film is known for. In truth, there's no more perfect seduction scenario than that of Tom Jones (Albert Finney) and Mrs. Waters (Joyce Redman) dining opposite one another, their eyes locked and never straying as they lick and caress, then nibble and finally suck and devour their food—then do it all over again, leaning passionately into every chicken leg and each juicy cluster of grapes.

Or, what about the scene in the 1988 romantic comedy, *Working Girl*[5], where Jack Trainer (Harrison Ford) and Tess McGill (Melanie Griffith) are sequestered in a small hot room, reviewing every detail of the merger they are about to pitch the next morning? The air is heavy; they are down to tank top (hers) and t-shirt (his) and glistening with sweat. He is nursing a cigar; she is licking perspiration off her upper lip. Their mouths are speaking only of the deal, but their minds are elsewhere entirely. Their eyes are fixed on one another as they move through Attention, Suggestion, Promise, Withholding, and back, with no possibility of realization while they try to keep their focus on the merger work. Suspended explosion hangs everywhere in the air between them.

The next day they remain in Withholding during the pitch meeting. But the previous night's mutual (agonizing!) seduction can no longer be staved off: As they descend the stairway in euphoria over their sold pitch, Jack grabs Tess and the next thing we know (we're not privy to the Attention, Suggestion, Promise and Withholding during the cab ride back to Jack's apartment), they are stumbling into Jack's apartment, flinging garments as they go.

> In *Working Girl*, Jack and Tess move through Attention, Suggestion, Promise, Withholding, and back. Suspended explosion hangs everywhere between them.

In even older classic films, seduction reigned; it was Hollywood's secret weapon in the box office! The studio moguls found ways to sneak seduction scenes in virtually everywhere, because they *worked*, and drew women in particular to the theater in droves.

Let's take a completely unlikely example—the wholesome family Christmas classic, *It's a Wonderful Life*[6] (1946), filmed during the era of the Hays Code (which started clamping down on sex in the movies around 1930). Now, you may think this is a odd film to use as an example of seduction par excellence, for there's not an iota of actual sex in the Jimmy Stewart/Donna Reed film (we can't count the scene where George unwittingly steps on Mary's robe and she dives naked into a bush, because we don't see anything). So there's no sex *per se* in the film, and yet the leading male not only flawlessly seduces his lady, he does it without *knowing* he's doing it, and without *wanting* to! (What a clever way of getting around that pesky Hays Code.)

In the scene, our hero George Bailey (Jimmy Stewart) is behaving terribly toward the lovely Mary (Donna Reed) as he painfully wrestles with his plans (to escape Bedford Falls and see the world) versus his libido (to pursue Mary). We can clearly see that George is desperately in love with Mary and wants her, yet at the same time, he also urgently wants to flee from a no-way-out future stuck where he is. In the meantime, Mary is forced to take a long-distance call from an admirer who is also a mutual friend of theirs. She is so confused by George's belligerent behavior that she tearfully muddles through the call. George continues to rage at and defy his feelings for her yet, all the while, he cannot take his eyes from her. Their faces and bodies draw closer and closer as she goes on with the call, his conflicting anger and need for her swelling as she struggles with her bewilderment and love for him. Closer and closer they are pulled to one another, imperceptibly, until at last he grabs her, hard, crying "Mary! Mary!" He kisses her feverishly and buries his face in her hair, sobbing; the telephone receiver falls from her grasp. Together, George and Mary dissolve in tears and love. *And both are clearly lost in their lust.*

> Oddly enough, there was never more effective use of seduction-to-'climax' than in the classic family film, *It's a Wonderful Life.*

Never was there a more effective use of riveted Attention, inevitable Suggestion, Promise Withheld and then—climax! (Or, at least, what amounts to the old Hollywood version of a climax, during the Hays Code era.)

Seduction *Works*

It's not by accident that my film examples all predate the last turn of the century—by decades! Lost in so much recent filmmaking (and in our culture, in general?) is that lovely delay of gratification that underlies all great seduction, as more current cinema heroes and heroines jump in and out of bed together like Mexican jumping beans—and sometimes leave us yawning. The powerful message in the older films? *Seduction works, and women love it!*

Be aware, however, that in the examples above, the characters didn't plan their seductions; they were presented with *opportunities* that were ripe for seduction. So keep your antennae up! Exploit seductive settings and opportunities by Promising and Withholding, at the very least. If you relearn how to make your sweetheart feel truly womanly and wanted by being worth your determined seduction efforts, she'll dress pretty for you, flirt with you, *und*ress pretty for you, and—best of all—she'll sleep with you again. Before you know it, you may even teach her to be so comfortable with seduction, she'll seduce you right back. And she'll do it all because she *wants* to. Try it and see.

Chapter 15
What's Her Fantasy?
(And Why You Should Care — a LOT)

You've sexually reconnected with your darling at long last, you're enjoying some welcomed intimacy once again and, as your gal has become more secure that your sexual feelings are directly linked to your feelings of love for *her*, you've even dipped your big toe in the waters of seduction with some interesting results!

At this point it should be crystal clear to you that we women are first and foremost turned on by our own impressions about your attitudes and behaviors toward us, swimming about in our charming little brains. Those impressions mean everything to us and (no matter what your own male brain would prefer to believe) *that's* what sparks our fires.

Did I say, our impressions about your attitudes and behaviors? I meant: your attitudes, behaviors, and your *words*.

> **Men don't understand that specific *words* ignite their woman's particular fantasies.**

So many men just have no innate sense of how critical and powerful what you *say* to us, is. Then, of course, there are those men who happily assert that they do indeed understand the power of words and their effect on women. These men routinely use words in their efforts to arouse their mates, and many are more than happy to be consistently verbal with their women.

The question is: *Do they know the right things to say?*

Like almost everything else men do to get their women into bed, men use the kind of "hot talk" that they instinctively know is a turn-on. And therein lies the problem.

> **To get women into bed, men may use the kind of 'hot talk' they instinctively know is a turn-on—and therein lies the problem.**

As with everything else we've discussed in this little book, so often the kinds of words and images that work for *a man* just don't work as well (or at all) for his female partner. And that's because *she is not a male*. She is not YOU!

Let me put it this way: If you have in the past used talk in sex, sexual foreplay, or *pre*-sexual foreplay (which I will always maintain is your most critical entrée to great sex), just what kinds of visual images have you painted with those words? Have you "instinctively" referred to your own feelings, your own body, your own erogenous zones, your own fantasies?

Hey, there's nothing necessarily wrong with that, especially if you happen to know that those kinds of mental images do indeed press your partner's particular sexual fantasy buttons (and especially if they turn up your own heat at the same time).

But what if they don't press her buttons? I mean, what if those kinds of uttered intentions are somewhat stirring to her on a certain level, but what if they don't *directly* ring her chimes? What if they miss, or are just left or right of the mark? Isn't that almost like being just left or right of her sweet spot? Don't you want to set her on *fire*, not just get her mildly interested?

To put it more directly: *If you knew exactly what to say to your woman to make her soar to the moon with you (and want to keep returning), wouldn't you SAY it?*

> **If you knew what to say to make her soar to the moon with you, wouldn't you say it? Why would you *guess* about what she needs to hear, when you could know for sure?**

Personally, I always wonder why men opt to *guess* about these kinds of things, when the very keys to their kingdom are right in front of them, just ready for the taking.

The fact of the matter is, you can whisper, utter or yell out any kinds of words or thoughts you imagine will get your lady excited. But you'd do so much better to use at least some of those words to refer to *her* very special fantasies, not just your own. What's more, if you have cleverly secured a mental "portfolio" of your woman's actual fantasies, then you'll always have a menu of mental images to choose from, instantly available for download. All you'll need to do is conjure them up for her at any given moment with whatever words, sounds (and then, actions) are pertinent.

Sounds brilliant, right? It is!

> **If you secure a mental 'portfolio' of her fantasies, you'll have a menu of images to instantly download. You'll then use whatever words, sounds and actions are pertinent.**

So, how do you find out precisely what her fantasies are?
There are four direct steps to finding out (and you should make use of each and every one of them):

1. **You immediately put aside your own preconceived notions** about what excites your woman (or any woman, for that matter). You open your mind to the possibility that

her fantasy may have nothing whatever to do with your own, and probably doesn't.

2. **You pay careful attention to her *daily* clues about her emotional needs,** for—surprise!—the innocent-sounding things she tells you during the course of any given day can be *directly* connected to her sexual needs. (You should also think back to the daily clues you may have missed up until now.)
3. **You pay careful attention to what she is actually *saying* to you during sex**—about what *she* needs, what turns *her* on, and what she hopes you will do *to* her. (That is, if you are still having any sex with her, or if you can remember back to what she used to say).
4. **You ASK her what her sexual fantasies are,** during a heart-to-heart "philosophical" conversation with her. (Do not skip this step!)

Let's look at how these four steps might work:

Step No. 1: Put Your Own Notions Aside

Okay, let's say, for instance, that other guys have always told you that a woman just loves to hear that a man's penis is rapidly expanding for her while he gazes at her great body and gets excited. Or, maybe (if you are not of the more explicit school of sexual discussion) you've always heard that a woman just wants to hear how hot for her you are, and hearing that revelation, all by itself, will get her home fires burning.

If her own particular sexual fantasy does revolve around watching a man get excited for her then, hey, your references to such an occurrence could certainly do the trick (literally). But have you used this approach in the past? Have you *assumed* that it worked for her because it sure as hell works for *you* while you utter words to that effect during or right before sex? Take a moment to think back about this: No matter how great *your* eventual climax was after the expression of such words, how responsive did *she* immediately become when you tossed out those descriptions? Did her breathing get heavier? Did she claw at your shirt and struggle to unbutton it? Did she urgently lead you into the bedroom and wrap her legs around you the first chance she got? Did she rub up against you like a she-dog in heat?

> **Did she urgently lead you to the bedroom and wrap her legs around you? Did she rub up against you like a she-dog in heat? If not, your magic words were for *you*—not for her.**

If she didn't do any of those things, then I'm afraid you didn't have the magic key after all, and you may have been too preoccupied with your own arousal, to notice it. The fact of the matter is, though you may not believe it (because you have no memory of her *ever* clawing at your shirt), the right words would have elicited reactions such as those I listed above. *Really!* And if you have trained yourself to believe that her simple act of allowing you to *proceed* with sex means that your words were effective for her, then you have been fooling yourself for quite a long time. Worse: You could be having so much more and better sex!

So, do you want simply to be *allowed* to have intermittent sex with the woman you love, or do you want her to *want* to have sex with you, every chance the two of you have to enjoy each other?

If your answer to the second half of that question was "Yes," then toss out your notions about which words and images probably turn her on, and *do not slide back to them* when you want to fire her up. Keep them in a mental box marked, "For Me to Use for *Me*, During Mutually Fabulous Sex," and bring them out for you to enjoy *after* you've learned to hit your partner's fantasy buttons.

Once your sweetie knows that you've got *her* number and have figured out how to use that information to make her crazy with desire (that information coming up next), she'll be more than happy to let you make yourself nuts with the words that you've always loved—and she'll be more than happy to oblige you with a few choice words of her own, to help elicit *your* fantasy, for *you*.

Nos. 2 and 3: Pay Attention to Clues (In Bed and Out)

Each and every day of your life with your lady, she is giving you vital clues about what she needs from you emotionally, in order to best relate to you in the man/woman part of your relationship (as opposed to the "equal partners" part of your relationship). For her, those man/woman relationship clues directly translate into how you will best relate to her in bed, and get her there in the first place. The truth is that her own vision of the man/woman aspect of her relationship with you, her partner, forms the basis of many of her sexual fantasies. Think about it: Does she seem to respond to the "all-powerful, all-knowing" side of you and disdain your more deferential moments with her? Is she at times a little girl looking for the hero in your to "rescue" her? Does she like to play the damsel to the villain inside "dangerous" you? Maybe she's got an impetuous side to her and has actually told you, at times, she needs you to be more "spontaneous" and less predictable and cautious?

> **Pay attention to the clues she reveals and then *feed them back to her daily*, to keep her fantasy 'sweet spot' primed.**

All you have to do is start to pay attention to all of these (generally abundant) clues. Then mentally note the things she is constantly revealing to you about herself, and *feed them back to her*—not just in bed, but daily—to keep her living her fantasy, and keep her primed for sexual interludes that hit right at the center of her fantasies the way a tennis ball hits a racquet's sweet spot.

As you pay more attention to your lady's clues, go ahead and jot some of them down and then connect those dots to her fantasy type(s). Then, on a daily basis, find ways to treat her *the way she is telling you she wants to be treated!* Sound confusing? It's not!

Check out the fantasy types below, their possible clues, and how you might feed her "type" with your own words and actions, in or (just as importantly) out of bed.

Command Me

Even if she is a powerhouse at work, effortlessly directing staffers and routinely making executive decisions, does she have a curiously opposite side to her nature when she is home with you, away from her "other" life? Does your Ms. Chief Executive, for example, like it when you talk baby-talk to her, or even call her "baby" when you are alone together? Does she seem happiest and most lovable when you are holding her close to your chest, surrounding her with your protective arms? Even though she can run a business with ease, does she seem to like it when you come to her rescue when little things around the house go wrong? (You kill spiders for her, jump in to save her from pipes that burst, hug her at night and tell her funny stories when she can't get to sleep). Does she even like to sit on your lap? Even though she routinely orders people about at work, does it appear to bother her or cause her to treat you less respectfully when *you* seem too deferential to her at home?

> **She may say, 'I need you to hug me,' or 'I need to feel you are taking care of me.' This woman may be turned on by a Commander.**

If a number of these things sound familiar to you, then your mate may see in you or need from you a strong "all-knowing" figure who she can look up to and who, though kind and benevolent, will keep a firm rein on her and not allow her to cross too many lines that, deep down, she'd rather not cross.

We can go into what's doubtless complicated Freudian psychology behind these particular needs, but this kind of feminine profile is so common that analysis doesn't really matter;

all *you* need to know is that you've got a woman on your hands who has to sense her man as strong and confident, and somewhat directive and powerful. You've got a woman who likes to be called "baby," likes you to direct the action and be decisive, and likes to be hugged like a little girl. Note it! *DO* it!

On a daily basis, play into her need by stepping back from any tendencies to defer to her. If you believe she is right about something, tell her confidently "Yes, I think you *are* right about that," and then move on. If she prefers one restaurant over another, consider the request and grant it or not, but don't always let this woman have her way or she will lose respect (and thus, sexual desire) for you. If she seems to love playing the little girl to your "stronger, wiser" persona, play the game with her whenever you can, in words and actions! Treat her like your precious little angel and take the reins to take care of her, but don't forget that this woman also needs your strength and self-assurance—even if it means verbally "disciplining" any bad behavior on her part, or bossing *her* around a bit, for a change!

When it comes to sex (and because a fantasy is *not* reality!) this kind of woman may not just want you to be strong for her, she may actually be turned on by being "commanded" by you to a certain extent. It's not that she doesn't want her mate to be sexually considerate (that is, not hurt or harm her), but she may get off on being told what to do and not be allowed to direct the sexual encounter herself. Why could this be such important knowledge for you? Simply because where your previously conceived notions of how to get her into bed with words and images may have revolved around telling her how much you'd like to drop your drawers for *her*, this kind of woman may be endlessly more excited by being ordered (yes, ordered!) to slip out of her panties for *you*.

Furthermore, if you take her *daily* cues into consideration, you will finally grasp that the hints themselves are an important part of her emotional makeup. She may very well have said to you, on many daily occasions, something like, "I need you to hug me," or "I like it when I feel you are taking care of me." In bed, she may even have said outright, "I love it when you tell me what to do," or she may seem frustrated by having to tell *you* what to do. For many women like the one described above, merely having to direct the action (when she really wants you to masterfully tell *her* what to do) is enough to mentally (and thus, sexually) distance her from it. If there are things she needs you to know (faster, slower, not so hard)— believe me, she will find a way to let you know. Commanding is only a fantasy, remember? It's play-acting! It's got everything to do with your masterful *attitude*; underneath the fantasy, you'll still be a considerate human being who has no intention of harming her or ignoring an important piece of feedback about the progress of the sexual activity.

> **If it's been your instinct to tell her what you want from her in bed, this girl's more sadistic fantasies may make your behavior a turn-off, and you don't even know it.**

Serve Me
There are myriad other types of clues you may encounter with women who tend to different kinds of emotional needs and, thus, fantasies. For instance, what about the woman who likes it when *she* is able to take the commanding role in your daily life together, and is happiest when your motto is "happy wife, happy life" or something to that more subservient effect? She may be modeling her parents' relationship, where her mother wore the pants. Or, she may be compensating for overbearing men she endured in her earlier life; who knows?

The good news is that she may want to take that desire to a whole new level in bed, via her favorite domination fantasy. She, may, in fact, be at her best when she is encouraged to be sexually powerful—even a little sadistic. If you are the kind of man who has always secretly suspected that black leather (for her) and handcuffs (for you) could be the greatest thing since sliced bread, then you may have ended up with the perfect sex partner—you just haven't been paying attention to her clues, or listening to what she has been trying to tell you.

For example, has she ever mentioned to you that it truly bothers her when she can't have whatever she wants whenever she wants it "simply because you should want her to be happy"? In bed, has she ever revealed that she really likes it when you "let her have her way with you," or when she can "make you crazy and you can't do anything about it"? If you truly care about this woman, you should be listening to these valuable clues and bits of information and, at the very least, using them to thrill both of you in the bedroom.

To get her warmed up for sex, you should be abandoning (at least for the time being), your natural instincts to tell *her* what you want from *her*. This kind of woman may immediately turn off to such instinctive requests on your part, perceiving them as just more control that *she* is expected to relinquish. Her response to such requests will, in the end, do you no good at all.

Suggestions about "servicing" *her* according to her every demand, however, may just set off the kind of response you both were hoping for. So, don't hesitate to give her the "How may I serve you?" treatment in any way you can muster, during any given day, even if it means bringing her lunch with a "Here you are, my darling mistress" and a subservient smile on your face. If she asks you to wash her car for her (while she directs your work, as usual), why not play *into* it this time and instead of resisting her commands, play-act with her! Then let her douse you with the hose (you're her slave *and* you're in a wet t-shirt; could it get any better for her?). If she requests your help with heavy boxes, don't respond with your usual, "Okay, but I'll have to do it later." Jump at your opportunity! This kind of woman may want to watch you flex your manly muscles and huff and puff for her—and all that manly servitude may serve *you* well, too, not long afterward.

Watch Me!

What about the woman who has tried to shock you with her extroverted tendencies every now and then? You thought you had married a demure little thing, but remember that time you were on vacation and she wore a see-through mesh top (with no bra), and then acted surprised when you calmly suggested she change before heading out to dinner? Has she in the past suggested kissing or hugging "where no one will see us" (but clearly could)? Or is your woman just the opposite: She's so conventional and concerned about what other people think of her (while openly expressing that she wishes she could throw abandon to the wind) that you've long suspected she's just dying to break free from her bonds? Either way, you might have a closet exhibitionist on your hands.

> **If the idea of having people watch naughty things being done to her is thrilling to her, what can you 'mention' during the week?**

Who knows how she got to be this way? The point is that the idea of people watching her do naughty things (or even better, having them watch naughty things being done *to* her), excites her beyond belief. Now, that doesn't mean that she actually wants to have you make mad, passionate love to her while your neighbors spy the action through your living room window. But it does mean that her fantasy—the *idea* that others could see her—is sexually thrilling to her. Therefore, anything you do to encourage that feeling during any given week will send her hormones into overdrive. You could merely *suggest* something outrageous to her in some highly conventional locale, and she'd have trouble getting it out of her mind until the two of you could actually be alone to act out your suggestion as though prying eyes were all around.

Not sure your lady falls into this category? Try this little experiment (but try it only if you have already reestablished sexual intimacy with her, and are actively loving your lady on a consistent basis): On a run-of-the-mill weekend, take her to the movies and, during a not-so-engrossing scene (after all, she wanted to *see* this movie), whisper to her that you can't stop thinking about doing [add anything you like here] to her, in the movie theater, while it's too dark for others to tell what you're doing. If she sighs audibly (in a good way) and then cuddles up to you, you can count your suggestion as a successful step in seduction, and suspect that you were on the right track about her fantasy type. If she runs with your suggestion and whispers back additional ideas along your original line, you were definitely on the right track. And if she takes your hand and proceeds to place it where you had suggested *you* would, you were not only on the right track, you should prepare yourself to be asked to leave the theater! (But it will be *so* worth it...)

Accost Me
You and your lady have been together for so many months, years or decades that (in real life) she's forgotten what it feels like to be approached by a complete stranger who clearly has something carnal on his mind. And for that she's glad—after all, she no longer has to deal with the lechers, creeps and stalkers she had to dodge and evade when she was out there alone in the world; you've taken her away from all that and she loves you for it.

On the other hand... Although she doesn't *really* want a random encounter with some weirdo in a bar somewhere, a make-believe One Night Stand with a mysterious stranger she'll never see again (and who she allows to do all sorts of unmentionable things to her) could be pretty darn exciting. As long as there's no real threat, danger, disease prospects or irreversible repercussions, that is. In other words, as long as the guy is imaginary, she can whip him up in her mind any time she wants or needs to, to make her real-life sex hot as can be.

Yet, what if you (the man she loves and feels safe with) happened to know about this particular sexual fantasy of hers, and could play into it simply by flipping off the lights on any given week night, lowering your voice to an unfamiliar tone, and whispering from across the room, "I've been watching you all night, lady, and I know you've been watching me, too. I don't care who you are or where you're from. All I know is that you're not leaving this room…" Better yet, what if you arrange to meet your sweetie at a bar neither of you have ever been to and *you* don't show up, but your alter ego, Mr. Mystery, does?

> **Though she doesn't *really* want a random encounter with some weirdo in a bar, a conjured One Night Stand with a mysterious stranger could be pretty darn exciting.**

The woman who would be thrilled off her barstool when you play into her favorite sexual fantasy scenario, may indeed have been a party girl way back when or even when you met her. She has probably mentioned to you more than once that although she loves her life with you (and wouldn't trade it for the world), she does sometimes miss the excitement of partying and bar-hopping, when a girl never knew what adventure the night might bring. She may be the daring type, generally, or she may even be the opposite: a woman who committed to a monogamous relationship when she was young, and so never had the chance to play with a little fire. Lately, she might be into Girls Nights Out, or even Las Vegas weekends with her (also happily committed) gal buddies, just to feel like a "chick" again, gamble, and have some fun.

If any of this strikes a chord—or even if you just suspect that her wings are feeling a little too clipped lately—start pretending to your lady that you're simply not the man she thought she was with. Pick her up from work on a friend's motorcycle. Call her at work and pretend you're a stranger who spied her in the elevator (just make sure she knows it's actually you). Take her out for dinner, dancing, gambling, playing pool, or to any type of place you've never taken her before, and tell her stories about yourself she may never have heard.

If you decide to delve a little deeper into her fantasy, it may indeed be time to play-act the real deal on a Saturday night, and set up a one-night stand for her with Dangerous Guy, the man in you she's never known (at least, not until now).

Pay Me or Enslave Me

So, you're secretly longing for a stripper pole in your bedroom? Well, you may have to wait a bit for the backorders to come through: These days, more stripper poles are being purchased by women than by the men who originally cornered the market for their own lairs. The ladies say the poles are all part of a new pole-dancing exercise craze, but methinks there's just a wee bit more to it. Women not only love to fantasize that they are strippers, but for centuries the most proper and refined women you can conceive of have delighted in imagining themselves as call girls, hookers, harem slave girls, courtesans, geishas, concubines, French maids, even as Playboy bunnies—any kind of woman who has found her way (or been kidnapped into!) a life of pleasing men in some sexual or sex-related fashion because she *has* to, in order to survive.

> **The most refined women have delighted in imagining they are hookers or harem slave girls—any woman in a life of pleasing men sexually because she *has* to, to survive.**

There are so many reasons that women count these kinds of fancies among their fantasy repertoires. In them, a woman is:

- **Paid (or enslaved) for her beauty** or desirability. It's not *her* fault she is so beautiful that men have to have her!
- **Forced to perform sexually.** It's not *her* fault that she had to learn to do all those dirty unmentionable things!

- **Summoned to perform sexually, day or night.** Basically, she's a sex slave whose life revolves around sex, sex, sex, and thus it's not *her* fault she's not raising children, running a business, cooking dinners, or coordinating PTA meetings—all the things she, alas, must do in real life.

Emotional needs that underlie other fantasies (secretly wanting to be commanded or forced; needing to be in a position of servitude; even exhibitionism) cross over into this age-old, cuts-across-all-demographic-boundaries fantasy. (Except perhaps the demographic of a woman who, in reality, is *in* one of the roles mentioned above, but even some professional call-girls admit to having fantasized about their trade before entering it.) So, to relate to your closet call-girl in daily life, refer to those preceding fantasy types and their cues listed above, and you'll have a good idea of how to act and speak to keep your girl's embers glowing. Then, of course, you could always bring her the kind of lingerie gift your Pay Me/Enslave Me gal would love to get any day of the week, and help her live the dream.

Men just love to dress their ladies for this fantasy, and almost all men, at one time or another, assume that their sweetie desperately *wants* to be a whore for them. Casually handing your honey a little shopping bag containing a red thong the size of an exclamation point may not the best way to go about encouraging this fantasy, however. (And you might want to ask her about this fantasy, first, in case it turns out to be a favorite one of yours, and *not* one of hers, after all.)

Other problems with outfitting your lady for this fantasy revolve around her size, weight and fit: If you buy her a gauzy little bra and panty set, but she is a 38DD and needs more underwire than the Brooklyn Bridge to hoist her up, she'll only be embarrassed to wear your little gift. (Likewise, the French shelf bra from Fredericks of Hollywood that you purchased for the gymnast you fell in love with, who only wears camisoles because there's just not enough cleavage for any kind of bra, let alone that one.)

What you *can* do, however is to paint a fiendishly depraved (call girl? geisha? harem?) scene for her with your wonderful words. You can even set up a time and place (that nice new motel down the street?), hand her a wad of (small) bills and order her onto the bed. (Just make sure no cops are lurking around.) And you can work up to the event, earlier in the day or the week (always the *best* way to warm up your woman), giving her plenty of time to costume herself for the occasion. Then, once you get a good glimpse at the boudoir getup she went for, you can gift her with something similar for her next "trick" or harem night. (Don't forget to check sizes and brand labels when she's not around; women often favor specific clothing lines and brands that complement their body type.)

> Don't focus on *your* part of the 'Pay Me or Enslave Me' fantasy first, or you may not get another crack at it.

Do remember, however, to focus on *her* part of the "Pay Me or Enslave Me" fantasy first, or you may not get another crack at it. If her fantasy is focused on all the wicked things her client, owner (or Sultan!) will be doing to *her* body, either let her get really into it before the focus goes back to you, or else use an act or two that she *must* perform on you first in order to get paid (and, of course, ravished).

Then pay her. Afterward, tell her that if she uses the dough to buy scarves for a Scarf Dance striptease, there will be more where that came from...

Force Me, etc.
Taking a number of these more playful fantasies to the next level—the "rape fantasy," as it's commonly called—is the woman who wants her sexuality more determinedly *forced* upon her and, as it is commonly believed, that includes more women than you might ever imagine. Once again, the motiva-

tions for this may be many: too guilty or well-raised to accept the depth of her own sexuality? A throwback to actual caveman times? No matter. The net-net on this is that she's praying you will one day figure out that she's turned on by being truly *compelled* to be your sex slave, against her better nature and in spite of her play-acting (not actual) flailing and protests. (Note: Always make sure the two of you have a safety word or phrase like "Uncle" that will stop the action in a flash if you are actually harming or scaring her.)

Of course, because in real life she loves and trusts you, she knows that you won't ever *genuinely* harm her or humiliate her in ways she wouldn't want to be humiliated (you'll have to carefully gauge the humiliation factor as you go along). And she trusts that *you* know that it's all a fantasy, carefully orchestrated to be passionate and in no way authentically frightening; just perfectly tailored for her, right down to her most explicit details (which you will draw out of her, the first chance you get).

> **She's praying you'll figure out she's turned on by being *forced* to be your sex slave, in spite of her (pretend) flailing and protests. She knows you won't *really* harm her.**

How will you know from more innocent daily cues that, on some level, your lady might be turned on by your whispered prospect of forced sex? This is a tough one, for the rape fantasy cuts across all types of women: confident and shy; brazen and reserved; sexually adept and sexually unskilled. I'd venture to say that most women who like to be sexually "commanded" in some way (our first scenario) probably also dream of the heavy-duty passion of a man being so carried away with lust for her that he must "take" her, consequences be damned.

And it's also quite common for women's fantasies to overlap, as well: A woman who fantasizes about being forced to make love, may also dream about being forced to make love *in public*. She may even fantasize about being forced to make love, in public, to *many men* at the same time! Or to men and *women*. (And we haven't even touched on those last two categories...)

To figure out how to relate, on a daily basis, to a woman who lists "Force Me" as one of her fantasies, it's a safe bet to say that you can go with the advice in the "Command Me" section, and just ramp it up a bit as you get close to the time when you are planning to help her carry out her fantasy. In other words, if you've got a plan in mind for Friday night, you might want to call her from the office earlier that day and play her besotted stalker, always keeping in mind that *her* rapist has forced *love*-making on his mind, not violence. Accordingly, your voice and words should suggest something closer to Fabio (the muscle-bound blonde model who graced the covers of so many hard-core romance novels), rather than some prison escapee about to scare the heck out of her.

As for additional fantasy types I may have omitted above (and most assuredly have), you'll just have to wing it, following general rules of listening to the clues she unknowingly drops, on a daily basis. The best news is that there are so many fantasies swimming about in women's brains that there are far too many to cover here. And all this time you thought *you'd* cornered the market on sexual reality shows of the mind.

No. 4: *Ask Her* about Her Sexual Fantasies
It's always so interesting to me when both men and women in long-term relationships admit that they've never actually asked each other about their deepest sexual fantasies. Since (conventionally speaking) the best time to have such a discussion is before, during or immediately after sex, I prefer to assume that such conversations didn't take place because the couple stopped having much sex before they became comfortable enough to have such an intimate conversation. In other words, they never had this important sex talk because their lack of a sex life made it dif-

ficult to have the discussion! (Sort of a not-screwed-if-you-do, not-screwed-if-you-don't situation!)

That's a shame, because the best way to find out anything from anyone is to just bite the bullet and ASK. And while you may feel that it was preferable to have the "What's your fantasy?" conversation when you were more sexual with each other, you need to have the talk anyway, and you need to have it as soon as possible.

> **Have the discussion about her fantasies! The good news is that she may have been *dying* to have it. The better news is that the talk itself could warm up some cold embers.**

The good news is that even if she is too shy to bring up this subject herself (and many women are), your lady may have been *dying* to have this discussion to tell you what, from her deepest recesses, she has so desperately wanted you to know. The even better news is that the very discussion itself, simply because it is about her fantasy (yes, it's finally "all about her"), may actually get some of those stone-cold embers warming back up again. After all, just putting words and images out there means she's got to envision her fantasy and bring it partially to life. Speaking of clever ploys!

Anyway, your job is twofold as far as the "fantasy" conversation is concerned:

1. **You'll need to make sure that the conversation is not too embarrassing for her**; also not too clinical, detached or superficial, which could make her feel uncomfortable. Keep it fun, light, and even sexy (like a little innocent phone sex, for example). This will be your one chance to make sure that you get her to drill down to the guts of her secret information, and you don't want to flub it. Then...

2. **Try to play down the importance of your own fantasies during this discussion**, even though you are presenting this talk as a *two*-way discussion (I'll tell you mine if you tell me yours). The process here is a little bit like espionage: You are trying to get the other side to reveal information, without revealing more of your own information than you need to. That's not to say that your fantasies (and their eventual fulfillment) are not important—they are equally as important as hers. But right now, your *primary* sexual fantasy is to have sex with your beloved again and, to coax her back, what you most need to know is how to make sex with you so *amazing* for her that she will want more and more of it. After you achieve that, she will want to know how she can make sex more amazing for *you*, and then you can tell her everything you like.

> A restaurant is the perfect place for 'The Talk.' She's dressed up, she feels womanly, she's got your full attention, and there's wine to loosen things up, just a bit.

So, for your heart-to-heart, pick a place where you are not needed by others and will not feel rushed; where you can have preliminary "philosophical" discussions about life and relationships (I know; a man's worst nightmare).

It may seem counterintuitive to have this kind of discussion at a good restaurant (with people, including wait staff, flitting about) but such a venue can be an ideal setting. For one, it means you've planned a nice night out with your honey. To a woman, that immediately means that the focus is on *her* (after all, you've taken her out for the evening and, hopefully, you are not distracted by things such as work, the kids, cell phones, etc.). Moreover, to her, an evening out to dinner is automatically an evening of conversation "about us" (with luck, still a favorite topic of hers).

Another reason a restaurant is a good bet: She's gotten dressed up for you, and that makes her feel womanly, which makes her more likely to feel sexy (or sexier than usual, anyway), and that makes her feel more willing to discuss your intimate relationship—or, at least, her own feelings about intimacy. A woman is more apt to discuss such things in this kind of setting than she is in the car on the way to little Lulu's tap dancing recital, or while she is trying to wind up a legal brief, for sure.

Finally, at a restaurant (unless you live in a dry town, or one or both of you is a recovering alcoholic), a little wine or a cocktail can definitely help this particular conversation along. I am not advocating alcohol if you are a teetotaler; and I am certainly not suggesting that the two of you polish off a fifth of Jack Daniels while you have this heart-to-heart—absolutely nothing will be gained by not recalling the information you so badly needed, or by getting her so drunk that her newly ignited flicker of sexual desire is doused (or soused, as the case may be).

But a nice restaurant with a small intimate table, some wine, a low level of background noise and music (just enough to mask your conversation from prying ears, yet not enough to make you shout "huh?" across the table), and a low turnover (so you are not rushed through your meal), is ideal.

> **Don't be afraid to fib and tell her you read an article about women's sexual fantasies and were surprised at how different they are from what you thought. Urge her to clarify!**

At some point, after some casual discussion about your recent life together or your relationship in general, you can take the direct route and let her know that you love her, miss her physically, don't want to pressure her about sex, but have always wanted to know what fantasies turn her on (and you'll file the information away for a future date; wink, wink). If she blushes or gets embarrassed, you can coax her charmingly with a "C'mon, we're in a restaurant—what can I do to you here? I'm curious; humor me!"

Or, you can take the less direct route, fib a little and, at some juncture in the evening, tell her that you were reading an article about women's sexual fantasies and were surprised at how different they are from what you had thought. You can say something like, "I know this sounds strange to be asking out of the blue, but I thought women just fantasized about movie stars they like, and stuff like that. This article talked about really specific things—like how some women like to be spoken to in bed, what scenarios they like their partner to paint—things like that. Is that true? I'm really curious. I'd really like to know…"

If you can coax her to admit that she doesn't know what *other* women fantasize about but only knows about her *own* personal fantasies, you'll be halfway to home. Just charm the information out of her (or bribe her with a night out doing something she likes to do that you don't), and she may open up. If she offers to "tell you hers if you tell her yours," go ahead and spill your guts. Just make sure you hit on the *concrete* things you are trying to get her to reveal as well: The precise words you like to hear (and why—how they make you feel about yourself); the positions you like (and why—how they make you feel about yourself); the scenarios that turn you on (you got it: and why—how they make you feel about yourself).

If you feel you need to, you can reassure her that we *all* have sexual fantasies of some kind, and we've relied on them all of our adolescent and adult lives. They are normal. And they aren't *reality*—we all know that. But they are very important, intimate clues to reveal to a love partner we trust (or wish to trust). Tell her that you will respect the information and always count yourself so lucky that she chose to share her most private fantasies with you.

The point is: Her fantasies are a vital part of her sexual machinery, with ideas and images that have most probably been working for her for many years (just as yours have, for you). And they do not mean that she needs more than you alone, to get her excited (do NOT sulk about that three-way fantasy she just revealed), or a man *other* than you (likewise, no sulking about the Brad Pitt scenario). Unless she tells you otherwise, her visions are pure fantasy, so you can be fairly assured that she doesn't *really* want to be gang-raped by a horde of men in a tent in an Arabian desert...

> **Don't just get the info; get ALL of it. Every great scenario has players, locations, costumes and lines. Coax, beg or wheedle, but get the lowdown and change your life.**

The important thing is: If the two of you have been together for any length of time and you haven't yet been able to glean some vital clues about her particular fantasies and then ask her about them outright, DO IT NOW! Stop guessing about these critical magic keys to her sexuality. Get the information. And while you're at it, get ALL the information—every great scenario has its players, locations, costumes and memorable lines. Her scenarios most assuredly do, too. Coax, beg (yes, for this you can beg), wheedle and bribe the info out of her. It may take more than one evening at a nice restaurant, but it will most definitely be worth it. Get the lowdown and change your life.

It's Always Your Choice

Once you have uncovered your sweetheart's most intimate fantasies or (if she will not directly reveal them to you), once you have deduced from her clues what direction they might take, it is entirely up to you whether or not you are comfortable creating sexual scenarios that will play to her desires. If you can now ascertain that your woman would probably love to be dominated in bed, but you're just not sure you can play the lustful, benevolent dictator to her poor little peasant girl (or even just masterfully order her about a bit), that's up to you. On the flip side, if you're the kind of man who must dominate and not be challenged by a woman, it may be difficult indeed for you to crawl on all fours while your lady (and her newly discovered need to dominate) rides you across the bedroom carpet, crying "*Yee*-hah!!"

Yet surely, somewhere along the way an understanding and a new way of respecting each other's needs can be negotiated. Sometimes, a change in attitude, tone of voice or style of caress can go a long way to helping someone get a little closer to what he or she needs. Imagination and a little extra effort can do wonders, too.

> **If you can't indulge her exhibitionist fantasy with a 'mile-high' on a real flight, whisper her through an imaginary one while you watch an airplane scene together on TV.**

For instance, if it turns out that your lady has exhibitionist tendencies and your sense of decorum simply cannot indulge her with a Mile High Club[7] interlude on your next flight to Austin, then why not take her on an *imaginary* mile-high rendezvous by whispering her through the entire setup one night, while the two of you are watching a *Mad Men*[8] episode with an airplane scene? As her eyes follow the screen, you can lean over and whisper, "See those empty seats near the back of the plane? I'm imagining that you and I are passengers, and we're sitting in those seats with a blanket across our laps, while the stewardess attends other passengers right alongside us. It's 1962 and, underneath that blanket, you're wearing a skirt, a garter belt and stockings. Let's Tivo[9] this thing, sweetie, and I'll describe what I'm doing to you under that blanket, while the stewardess pours coffee for that man across the aisle…"

As I've said, you can do what you want with the information your girl reveals to you directly or indirectly. But if you work hard to (at long last!) uncover her unique sexual fantasy keys, it will be a shame to let them remain between her ears.

When Fantasies Don't Jibe, and Other Dilemmas

So, after dutifully working through the Four Steps I've described, it turns out that her fantasies are all about dominating. Unfortunately, yours are, too. How can both of you be the rider when no one wants to be the horsey?

You can take turns. And maybe even discover something that you never suspected you might enjoy or at least think is, well, interesting. Once again, negotiating is the key here. If you're just not into whips and chains, suggest that she initiate you gently and introduce you to her more dominant side by way of silk scarves, loosely tied to the bedposts. The next time, you *both* can "lead" the action if yielding to any type of authority is a turn-off for her. This way, she'll finally get her honest-to-goodness fantasy life with you in the bedroom. And in between her every other fantasy session (now that you understand her better), you'll be so happy to have her back in bed that you won't even care that you both want the Commander role.

> Look at your newfound knowledge about her *daily* emotional needs from you, as GOLD. They are the clues that will lead you right to her most potent sexual fantasies.

The truth is that many men insist they will be happy to do almost *anything* in bed, as long as there's *any* kind of sex, and your sweetheart may be thrilled to discover that you are more than pleased to give her her way more often than not—as long as there *is* a way. Any way at all!

As for your newfound knowledge about her *daily* emotional needs from you, and how they affect her sexual arousal, look at this knowledge as GOLD. If it turns out she likes and needs to dominate, just negotiate a wee bit and ask her not to do it around your friends. Then tell her that you will happily wipe down the floor on your hands and knees on Sunday afternoon while she barks orders—as long as she does it in black panties and bra, wearing heels. (You could manage that, right?)

And if the lack of drama in your (nice, peaceful) life is making your little drama queen crazy while it keeps you ulcer free, learn to "faux fight" a little: raise your voice now and then, wrestle her onto the carpet and give her a thrill. Once you understand what it is that your woman needs, for goodness' sake find *some* way to oblige her with a few tweaks in attitude, behavior and words.

Maybe you've recently discovered that you have actually married a little girl hiding inside that killer attorney. You've read her daily cues well and have even gotten her to reveal her deepest fantasies to you. You now know that—despite her behavior to the contrary—she doesn't want a "yes" man at all; she secretly pines for a caveman! This knowledge might possibly do you a whole world of good, convincing you to be the guy that you, too, always wanted you to be.

Give it a shot: Tweak daily words and actions wherever you can, to set off the kind of response you may not have seen from your lady for a long, long time. If you've done a good job, you'll find yourself back where you've so longed to be and you can quickly negotiate fantasy give-and-take in your bedroom—the place where you both can be who you *really* are, with everyone paying attention and no one assuming that they got it right "by instinct."

Chapter 16
Your Tick List:
The 15 Fundamentals

I have to say, you've been quite amazing, making your way through this book from cover to cover, in your determined and dedicated effort to change your life with your lady and lure her happily back into bed! At this final juncture, I hope you can appreciate how essential it has been to get inside that upside-down little head of hers to uncover what makes her libido tick—for that's where sex and love and everything in between begins for her: right there in that little noggin.

Of course, you'll never remember every single thing we've talked about here, and no one expects you to. It's been most important to introduce you to a different way of *thinking* about sex with your woman, and what may be affecting her reticence to rock and roll with you. It's been most important to introduce you to some new *concepts*; notions that just may never have occurred to you.

Now, though, because you're a man—a logical, action-oriented problem-solver by nature—you will need to devise your action plan. (*How will I proceed to get my sweetie back into bed? What will be my first type of step? What might come next? What should I remember—at all cost—not to keep doing?*) Only you can apply what you've learned here to your specific lifestyle with your mate.

And because you're a man (and no man in his right mind heads into the fray without some kind of "tick list," be it jotted or mental), I leave you with the following memory joggers, to help you through. You won't find everything discussed herein, but the bare-bones basics that follow will help you, whenever your mind or resolve wanders, to hearken back to the nuances of many of our discussions. Hopefully, the little list below will keep you on your unwavering path back toward the darling girl you charmed and won and convinced to make a life with you—a life full of love and wonderful, glorious sex.

Stay the course, and remember your 15 Fundamentals!

1. **She Is Not *You*,** and she is not sexually motivated by the things that drive you. If she were, she'd be looking at porn sites instead of reading romance novels.
2. **Sex = Love, Love → Sex.** To you, sex *means* love. To her, love *moves* her to sex.
3. **Love is Active Only.** *Saying* you love her doesn't feel like love to her. To her, love means your *actions* and *behaviors*. Learn to actively love her *first*.
4. **Remember: It's Response!** You're already "wired into" sex, but she needs things to respond to, to get her hormones pumping. Give her what she needs! Don't be "relationship lazy," or you'll pay the no-sex price.
5. **Don't Ask, Don't Expect.** In her eyes, asking for sex puts *her* in the decision-maker position and thus weakens *you*, instantly changing the male/female dynamic. "Expecting" sex (*But it's Saturday night!*) gives her zero to respond to, which means no heat-up for her.
6. **Angry Women Don't Have Sex.** Maybe *you* can compartmentalize, but if *she's* angry, you're not getting any. Learn how to defuse the anger by changing your mate's perception of you.
7. **End Magical Thinking.** Put an end to "Magical Thinking" (*I'm sure she'll understand about the game; that I didn't have time for a decent gift; if I can't go out with her friends;* etc.), if you ever want to have great sex again.
8. **Value = Sex.** She wears your value of her for all the world (especially other women) to see. Your sex life with her will be directly proportionate to your "active" valuing of her.

9. **Beauty = Sex.** *Never underestimate beauty insecurity!* Even film stars are insecure about their looks—yes, *really*. And a woman who does not feel beautiful cannot make you happy in bed. Learn how to make your girl feel truly lovely, and get the sex life of your dreams.

10. **Build the Bridge to Bed.** Learn to "connect and engage" with her and you'll keep open the bridge that goes directly to your bed.

11. **Take Back Your Power—Or Else.** You want respect, and she *wants* you to take back your strength and power. Change your dynamic quickly and permanently.

12. **The Nearness of You is a Drug.** Never underestimate the heady power of male "nearness." She needs it desperately and it's so easy to give her. The more masculine *you* are around her, the more feminine *she* will feel—and that leads straight to sex.

13. **Chase Her Right Into Bed.** If you want the kind of sex you've dreamed of, re-learn to pursue her. Don't wait for (or expect) her to come to you. Go *get* her!

14. **Any Man Can Master Seduction.** If you want the kind of sex every man pines for, learn the art of seduction.

15. **Help Her Live Her Sex Fantasy—and You'll Get Yours.** If you want your woman to want you as she never has before, uncover her sex fantasy "type" from her daily words and behaviors, and you'll make both of your dreams come true. Forever.

Appendix
Not Tonight; Headache.

Is it possible that your lack of a sex life has nothing at all to do with you, and is all about your lady love feeling crummy? The larger part of this book is not focused on such a potential root cause of no-sex-itis, because over a period of months or years, health conditions ordinarily ebb and flow (and yet, the frequency of your sexual activity has been mostly *ebbing*). What's more, women tend to be a good deal more complicated than backache = no sex for five years. But since anything is possible (and since there are so many physical conditions that notoriously sap sex drive for women), please do *not* neglect to read on.

Below is vital information you simply must take to heart before you undertake your new mission to rebuild your love life, for the issues below can already be dramatically impacting the current low-sex status of your relationship with your mate. These are factors that could absolutely be contributors to her reticence, and you should certainly consider them. They are:

Health Issues
It may be possible (heck; it's *probable*) for a man to valiantly bed his woman even as his own health is challenged, but most women are not put together that way. Once again: *We are not like you!* The fact of the matter is, our sexual function (with its delicate balance of female hormones) is intricately tied to the state of our health. Many women simply cannot function sexually when their health is in a less than optimal state. So, if you are truly serious about dramatically improving your sex life with your mate, you must somehow find a way to make sure your sweetheart is attending to her health issues. At the very least, find a way to make sure she has a thorough routine check-up. Issues such as hormonal imbalances, low thyroid function[10], diabetes and other chronic

diseases (which could be going undetected), low blood sugar, PMS/PMDD[11], frequent migraines, low blood pressure, weight gain, underlying infections or inflammation, depression, even vitamin deficiencies can *dramatically* dampen a woman's libido—sometimes permanently, particularly if she does not secure medical care.

Why not tell your sweetheart that you are going for your own check-up, and suggest she schedule hers at the same time? Or, change or update your family insurance policies (life, health etc.) so that she will have to be checked out by a medical professional. Or, suggest the two of you try a new birth control method (which ordinarily would require she visit her gynecologist). Or, declare that it's time to join a gym together (which may require physical exams). Or—and here's a luverly idea for you both, provided you have some ready cash available—plan a weekend spa stay that includes an initial on-site physical exam (or else requires a physical beforehand).

The fact is, there are any number of ways to gently prod your beloved into taking better care of herself, and if none of the above common-sense approaches work, you can always take the loving, caring, personal approach: Sit down with her, hold her little hand in yours, look lovingly and determinedly into her eyes, and (*without* mentioning your own lack of sex) declare that you are concerned about how she has been feeling. Tell her you want her to have a thorough check-up to make sure that she is all right—and you'll even go with her and sit in the waiting room and read four-month-old women's magazines and then take her out to lunch afterward.

If she's concerned about the cost of a full medical exam, or she has limited or no medical coverage, go ahead and offer to pony up the cash for a routine physical offered through her workplace or a reputable walk-in clinic. Just make sure to insist that it include a basic blood panel (lab work) which might reveal latent problems that could be silently damaging her health. That's how much you love her and want her to feel better.

Weight Gain

Just as with sexual disinterest, weight gain, too, can be directly attributable to underlying medical conditions (underactive thyroid and diabetes are only two of many culprits). Or, your lady may be using food to deal with stresses in life that she's having trouble handling. The daily stresses of working, running a household, raising kids and still trying to be a woman and have some kind of life with her mate are enough to send many women right into the pantry for a bag or two of potato chips. And, unfortunately, women are often less likely than men to use physical activity (golf, basketball, bicycling, for instance) to handle stress.

Is her life just not that stressful, as far as you can see? Boredom, too, can be a direct cause of overeating. The fact of the matter is that (even though we ate like little birds when you were dating us), we girls just love to chow down, and our bodies, with weight-producing hormonal-balance problems that you guys just don't have, get fat quickly—especially when we have too much time to hang around coffee joints sucking back double lattés with extra whipped cream.

Then, effectively plumped to a nice Rubenesque roundness, we'll try to hide our bodies any way we can, so that you can't see how chunky we've become. And if we're trying to hide in oversized tops (or your sweats), we're certainly not going to let you see us *naked*. And if we're not going to let you see us naked, chances are *your* chances of a roll in the hay are going to be greatly reduced.

Nowadays, there are plenty of women who don't wear a size 8 who are quite happy to strut their stuff and are proud of their size E-cup breasts and their 46-inch hips. Our rapidly "enlarging" societal weight expectations are enabling a real change in attitude where queen-sized women are concerned.

But your lady may not be one of the confident ones and, if that's the case, your sex life will remain on hold until she gets control of her weight and her body returns to a size she feels pretty (and sexy) in. Don't try to understand why you must be relegated to months without sex as she struggles with her weight issues. Just help her get assistance, if she asks for it. If she doesn't ask you for help, consider speaking to her parent, sibling or good friend about suggesting visits to a weight control clinic or program. And if neither of you can seem to confront the issue head-on, make sure to tell her that she is *always* beautiful to you, even with a few extra pounds. Then see what she says (or duck). But *address* it. Don't leave the situation as the elephant in the room, or expect the issue to magically disappear—*if* you ever want to have sex again.

Exhaustion
Depending upon what's going on in her life (new job, young children, dealing with elderly parents, etc.), your girl may be going through a stage where's she so pooped she's having trouble with snap, crackle and pop.

> **Women don't have the same internal alarms men do, warning: 'Nap now. Read paper now. Leave lawn care for later.' We just keep pushing until we are spent.**

Certainly, there are plenty of times when we women are a bit fatigued from a trying day, yet we still can be effectively lured into sex. But when it comes to *profound* exhaustion (ongoing lack of sleep or days and weeks of being overtaxed), females simply are not like the male of our species: he can be ready for action any time, any place, in any condition imaginable.

[I wish I could tell you how many times I've innocently informed my husband that I had been longing for him at 3 a.m., but knew he had an early call the next morning, and so back-burnered my impulses for a more conducive time. To which he responded incredulously, "Wha-a-t?? Why didn't you wake me?" To which I stammered back, "But you told me you had to get up at 5 a.m. and needed to get to bed early for a good night's sleep—" To which he retorted, "I've told you, that doesn't apply to SEX!"]

Clearly, there's a very real disconnect between the genders when it comes to feeling spent. Women, in general, can exhaust themselves far beyond their physical—and, importantly, emotional—reserves simply because they wear so many hats: wife, mother, lover, breadwinner, chef, chauffer, housecleaner, laundress, sports enthusiast, community activist, blogger, 24/7 friend, and on and on and on... And, to make matters worse, for some reason women do not have the same internal alarm mechanisms that men do, warning us when we are on the way to depleting our reserves. Or maybe we just choose to ignore that little voice that says: "Nap now. Read paper now. Go to gym now. Leave the dishes, dog and lawn care for later." Instead, we just keep pushing and pushing ourselves until somewhere down the line, we collapse. And so our physical and mental exhaustion deepens and can last for a few hours, a few days or (God help our husbands and boyfriends) months or *years*.

Once again, this is not to say that the advice contained in this book will not provide true relationship improvements which can help to relieve some of the exhaustion your sweetheart may be experiencing (and which is directly impacting the lack of physical intimacy between you. The mind-body connection is indeed a mysterious and powerful link).

Take Action
In the meantime, however, you will need to consider health, weight and physical/mental exhaustion issues either before you launch your back-to-bed initiative, or at least at the same time that you are putting your new action plan on the board. That is, if you are serious about reestablishing the love life the two of you have lost, or achieving a level of sexual closeness you may only have dreamed about.

The point is: When it comes to health, weight and exhaustion issues, YOUR WOMAN IS NOT LIKE YOU. (Yes, that *is* the mantra of this book.) She genuinely may not be able to function sexually when her health is suffering, when she is overweight, or when she is feeling "used up" by the daily demands of her life. You, Mr.

Problem Solver, can do much to help her resolve these three issues, and the easiest of the group to resolve is deep-seated fatigue.

Here again, sit down with her. Tell her you love her. Tell her you can see that she is feeling worn out and over-extended. Tell her that you are deeply concerned and will do whatever it takes to help her scale back. Assess the situation with her.

Find solutions that don't just make sense to *you*, but that will work for *her*. (And pay attention: She may not wish to give up her blog or her time with her girlfriends, but she might happily give up doing your laundry, cooking a full five nights a week, or holding down that second job.) Don't get your back up! Be realistic: You *want* her to retain the activities that refresh and renew her and that keep her vital and interested in the world around her—that's part of what keeps a woman sexy and appealing! It may *not* be in your best interest that she feels like a scullery maid and chauffeur. It *might* be worth $50 to the two of you to hire a housecleaner every other week. It *might* alleviate her weekend exhaustion if you were to run the kids to basketball and tap dancing on Saturday morning—especially if a rested and relaxed woman is awaiting your return *in bed*.

> **She's not like you: She may not be able to function sexually when she's pooped or unwell. Don't take it personally—
> DO something about it!**

Look carefully—and honestly—at these issues. Go back in your mind and try to recall how many times in the past month she has mentioned that she is tired or not feeling very well. After weeks, months (or years) of such complaints, it is indeed possible that you are tuning them out and perceiving them as complaints about *you*. ("If I'm such a good husband/boyfriend/mate/provider, then why is she always tired and feeling crummy?") Get over it! This is not about YOU. Your sweetheart may be desperately trying to tell you something about HER. All this time, she may have been begging for your help. IT IS NOT PERSONAL—at least, it wasn't in the beginning.

Now, though, she may very well be upset that you have not been paying attention to her and have tuned her out. So, take her willingness to continue to try to let you know what is impacting your life together (and, importantly, your sex life), as a gift.

No one is asking you to relieve her of all obligations or costs, to help her with her issues. But do start paying attention, getting interested, and helping her to get back on track. You'd do it for a good buddy who needed help, wouldn't you? Then by all means, do it for the woman you love.

Deep-seated Relationship Problems
If it's been months or years since you've had any sense of the crosses your gal is bearing, or if it's been years since you've cared (primarily because your relationship is overrun by resentment on both sides), then you've got major issues that, again, must be attended to first, or at least *along with,* the back-to-bed measures you are about to undertake. Otherwise, your sex life improvement will be all uphill.

And that's because while *you* may say that you can keep relationship difficulties and sex entirely separate (and, frankly, most men cannot keep them entirely separate—at least, not with the same woman), your mate most *definitely* cannot keep such matters separate (at least, not with the same man).

During your relationship struggles or even during long periods of infrequent sexual interaction with your mate, you may have shared some memorable "angry" or make-up sex with her. Yet, if you think about it, the rest of your intimate interactions (if they exist) have probably felt more like robotic walk-throughs. It is difficult indeed to keep underlying resentments and recriminations from eroding the stable physical life you may once have shared.

It's important to know, however, that many of the deep-seated problems that exist between men and women in relationships hearken back to basic misunderstandings about the opposite sex, and this book can dramatically improve that quickly. But if your relationship has regressed to the point that you hate the sight of each other or will never, ever forgive each other for the ways you have treated children, family, friends, finances and what-not, then while you are considering the methods in this book, also dedicate yourself to finding a family therapist or marital counselor who can help you open and reestablish the lines of communication.

> **Many of your problems may hearken back to misunderstandings about the opposite sex. But if you hate the sight of each other, reopen communication channels.**

In short: Suck it up. Bury your pride and ask friends, family and coworkers (who may have gone through similar difficulties) which therapists they might recommend. Personal referrals are always best. Or, query your family doctor or religious adviser about counselors. You can also head to a reputable resource such as your local faith-based or interfaith family services, or to an online referral service such as *Psychology Today*'s "Find a Therapist" listings (www.psychologytoday.com), designed to help you review specialties and credentials of professionals in your area.

If you take an honest look at your relationship as a whole and cannot deny that it is in serious trouble, seek out a place where you and your mate can attempt to communicate honestly—this time in the presence of an unbiased and trained professional who can help guide you. My very best recommendation for you is that famous Nike® advice that has (believe it or not) changed so many lives:

Just Do It.

Notes

1. Stritof, Bob and Stritof, Sheri. "Poll Results: Do You Have a Low Sex Marriage?" About.com. Retrieved 21 May 2012. <http://marriage.about.com/> 1
2. Gray, John. *Men Are from Mars, Women Are from Venus*. New York: Harper Collins, 1993. 80
3. Carmichael, Hoagy and Washington, Ned. "The Nearness of You" 1938. 89
4. *Tom Jones*. Dir. Tony Richardson. Perf. Albert Finney, Susannah York, Hugh Griffith, Edith Evans. Woodfall / United Artists, 1963. 113
5. *Working Girl*. Dir. Mike Nichols. Perf. Melanie Griffith, Harrison Ford, Sigourney Weaver. Twentieth Century Fox Film Corporation, 1988. 113
6. *It's a Wonderful Life*. Dir. Frank Capra. Perf. James Stewart, Donna Reed, Lionel Barrymore. Liberty Films, 1946. 114
7. Mile High Club™. "The term *'Mile High Club'* refers to two people engaging in sexual activity (sexual intercourse) at an altitude of no less than 5,280 ft (a mile high above the earth) in an airplane." <http://www.milehighclub.com> 139
8. *Mad Men*. Creator Matthew Weiner. Perf. John Hamm, Elizabeth Moss, January Jones. Lionsgate/AMC. 2007-2012. 139
9. TiVo® is a registered trademark of TiVo Inc., or its subsidiaries worldwide. 139
10. *Low thyroid function* refers to any diseases or chronic conditions such as hypothyroidism (underactive thyroid), Hashimoto's disease, benign tumors or malignant cancers of the thyroid, undiagnosed or sluggish thyroid, etc. An excellent resource of information about sex and the thyroid (and other aspects of underactive thyroid) is *Solved: The Riddle of Illness* by Stephen E. Langer, MD, and James F. Scheer (McGraw-Hill), 2006. 145
11. *PMS/PMDD* refers to the disorders *Premenstrual Syndrome (PMS)* and *Premenstrual Dysphoric Disorder (PMDD)*. *PMS* comprises a constellation of symptoms that are said to occur 5-11 days prior to menstruation, and which can include physical and emotional symptoms such as bloating and discomfort, irritability and mild depression. *PMDD* is a more extreme form of *PMS* and can include extreme tension and severe depression. While *PMS* is fairly common among menstruating women of all ages and ordinarily dissipates after the onset of a woman's monthly period, *PMDD* is believed to affect only 3 to 8 percent of menstruating females. *PMDD* symptoms may linger beyond the onset of monthly menses. Over-the-counter medications are generally prescribed for *PMS*; *PMDD* usually requires medical care. 146

About the Author

Stephany Ekman has been studying the "dance of the sexes" for two decades, in preparation for this book. A professional how-to writer, she has made her career in helping people to work, play and love better. She has two children and lives out West with her husband and their wire-haired terrier, Bogus.

www.ingramcontent.com/pod-product-compliance
Lightning Source LLC
Chambersburg PA
CBHW071506040426
42444CB00008B/1512